Science Panorama 7

Biology

Series Editors
Meenakshi Atal
Manjuli Mukherjee

Collins

Science Panorama 7

Biology

Series Editors

Meenakshi Atal

Manjuli Mukherjee

Preface

Science Panorama is a series of books for Classes 1 to 8, which includes 3 books each for Physics, Chemistry and Biology for middle school. The middle school series has been updated based on the **new syllabus** prescribed by the **Council for the Indian School Certificate Examinations**. In line with the new syllabus, a thematic, coherent and structured approach has been followed and all the new topics suggested in the syllabus have been included. Chapter-wise worksheets have also been provided to effectively integrate subject knowledge and life skills for overall development.

This updated edition also emphasizes on developing scientific skills such as observation, investigation, analysis, research and other inferential skills. It focuses on development of concepts as well as their application in real life. Sufficient examples from everyday life have been provided to help learners understand the concepts using age-appropriate language. Colourful illustrations and well-labelled diagrams have been included to engage learners and aid their understanding.

Some Key Features

Science in Context: Additional information on the topic being taught

Do You Know? Interesting facts related to the given topic

Greenathon: Some tips to keep the environment clean and green

Challenge Yourself: Questions testing students' ability to reason and extrapolate

Activities: Individual/collaborative activities to hone experimental and deduction skills

Know the Scientist: Famous scientists and their contribution to the topic at hand

Revision Zone: In-text questions for assessing progress in the course of learning

Keywords: Important words from the chapter along with their definitions

In a Nutshell: Summary of the chapter content

Mind Map: Flowchart for quick recapitulation

Exercise: Variety of questions given at the end of each chapter

Subject Integration Worksheets: To effectively integrate knowledge across subjects

Life Skills Worksheets: To create awareness, empathy and a positive attitude towards self and others

Assessment papers: Two assessment papers at the end of the book for effective evaluation

We would like to take this opportunity to thank all the teachers who reviewed the books and provided their valuable feedback, which helped in improving the quality of the content.

Any suggestions or constructive criticism from the users are welcome. We shall try to incorporate those in the future editions.

Authors

Key Features

Do You Know?

Interesting facts related to the given topic

Do You Know?

Earth is estimated to be around 4.5 billion years old. The first life form is estimated to have appeared around 3.7 billion years ago.

Science in Context

Additional information on the topic being taught

Science in Context

Some people have only 28 teeth. The remaining 4 teeth appear later during the age 17-21 and are called **wisdom teeth**. Some people do not have wisdom teeth at all!

Challenge Yourself

Questions testing students' ability to reason and extrapolate

Challenge Yourself

You have studied in Class 4 about microorganisms called viruses. They have not been included in any kingdom. Find out why.

Know the Scientist

Famous scientists and their contribution to the topic at hand

Know the Scientist

The concept of an energy pyramid was developed by **Charles Sutherland Elton** (1900-1991). He published this in his book *Animal Ecology*. These pyramids, ...erefore,

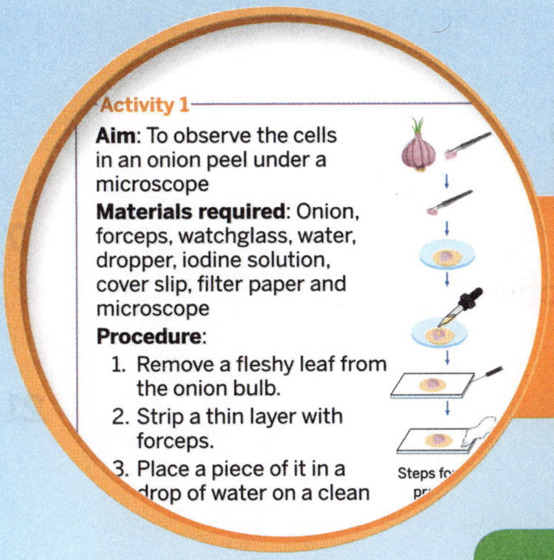

Activity

Activities to hone experimental skills

Revision Zone

In-text questions for assessing progress

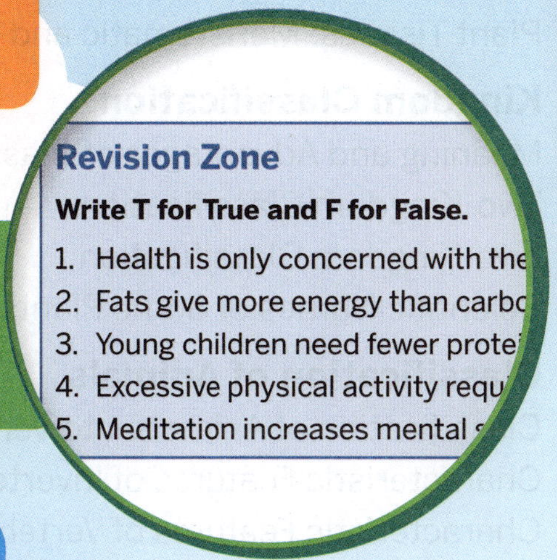

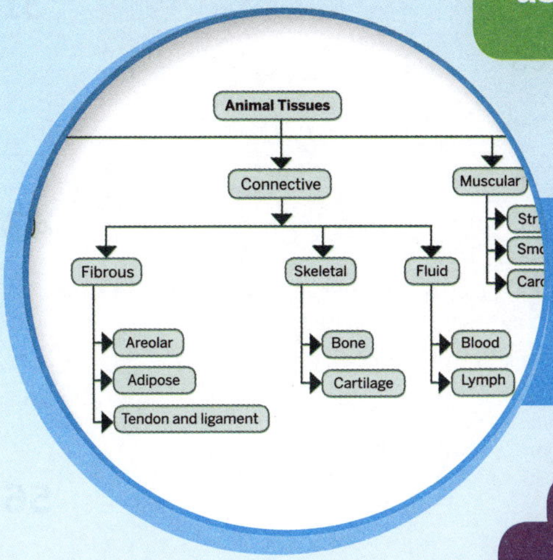

Mind Map

Flowchart for quick recapitulation

Exercise

Variety of questions given at the end of each chapter

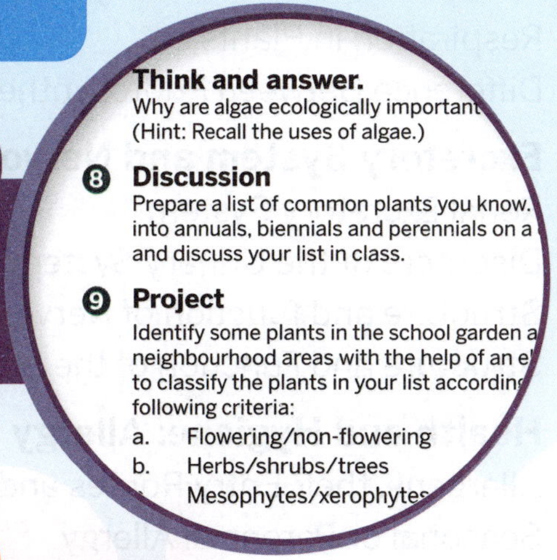

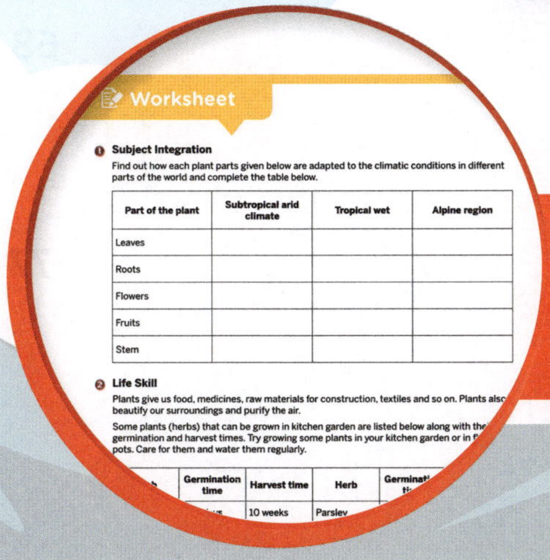

Worksheet

Thematic worksheets on integration of knowledge across subjects and Life Skills

Contents

Tissues

1

What I shall learn

- Animal tissues
  - o Epithelial tissue
  - o Muscular tissue
  - o Nervous tissue
  - o Connective tissue
- Plant tissues
  - o Meristematic tissue
  - o Permanent tissue
    - Simple permanent tissue
    - Complex permanent tissue

Introduction

In all multicellular organisms, groups of cells specialized to perform a common function form **tissues**.

For example, in animals, muscle cells that have the ability to contract and relax form the muscular tissue, and nerve cells that have the ability to conduct messages to and from the brain form the nervous tissue.

In plants, the cells of a bark form one type of tissue and the chlorophyll containing cells in the leaf form another type of tissue.

In this chapter, we will learn about the various plant and animals tissues, organs and organ systems.

Animal Tissues

Animal tissues can be grouped into four basic types: epithelial tissues, muscular tissues, nervous tissues and connective tissues.

Epithelial Tissues

- Epithelial tissues cover the entire internal and external surface of the body.
- They perform functions such as protection, absorption, secretion and sensory perception.
- The cells are found in layers and there is little or no space between adjacent cells.
- The nucleus is present towards the base of the cells.
- All epithelial tissues are separated from the other tissues with a thin layer of connecting tissue called the **basement membrane**.
- Basement membrane provides structural support while binding to the neighbouring structures.

Depending on the specific function, and the shape and size of the cells, epithelial tissues can be grouped into the following types:

- Squamous epithelium
- Cuboidal epithelium
- Columnar epithelium

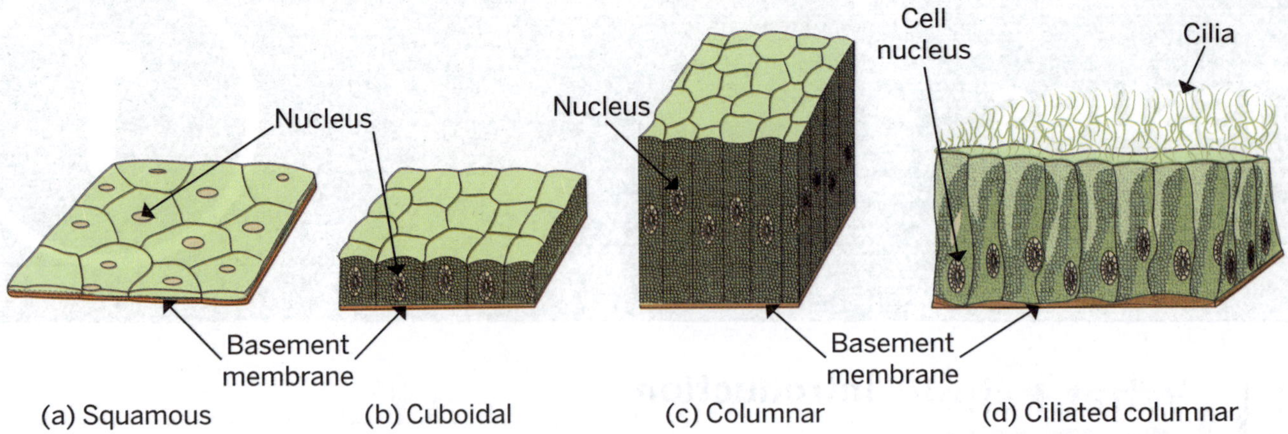

▲ Fig. 1.1 Epithelial tissue

Muscular Tissues

Muscular tissue is present in the muscles of the body. Muscles contract and relax to bring about movement of body parts in animals. They also provide mechanical support.
The human body is made up of more than 600 muscles.

Depending upon the structure and function, muscles can be grouped into three basic types: skeletal muscles, smooth muscles and cardiac muscles.

Skeletal Muscles or Striated Muscles or Voluntary Muscles

- These muscles are attached to the bones; hence, they are called skeletal muscles. They help in the movement of bones.
- The cells are long and cylindrical. They have many nuclei (plural of nucleus).
- The cells have alternate dark and light bands that give these cells a striated appearance. Therefore, they are also called striated muscles.
- These muscles are voluntary in action, that is, we can control their movement. For example, when we bend our arm, the striated muscles in our arm help us to do this.

Smooth Muscles or Unstriated Muscles or Involuntary Muscles

- The cells are spindle-shaped (thin and elongated) with a single large oval-shaped nucleus.
- The cells do not have bands or striation; hence, the name smooth muscles.
- Smooth muscles are found in the inner layers of the digestive tract, urinary bladder, uterus and blood vessels.
- All smooth muscles are involuntary. We cannot control the muscles of our stomach or blood vessels.

Cardiac Muscles

- Muscles specifically found in the walls of the heart are called cardiac muscles.
- They are special muscles that work non-stop without getting tired.
- Structurally, cardiac muscles are short, cross-striated muscles with numerous nuclei (like skeletal muscles) but functionally they are involuntary (like smooth muscles).

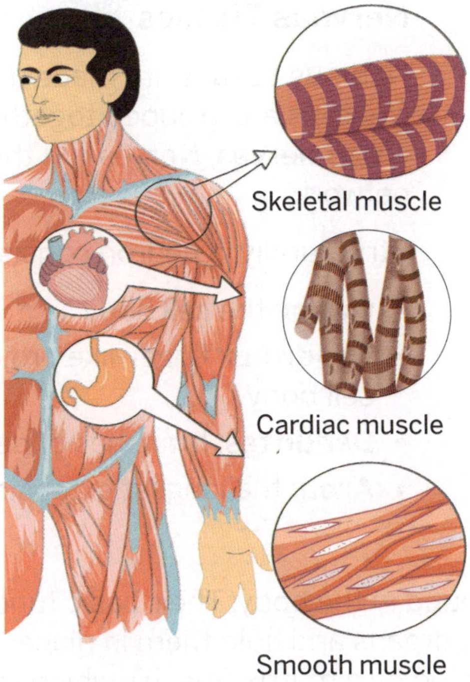

▲ Fig. 1.2 Types of muscular tissues

Table 1.1 Types of muscles

Muscle	Skeletal muscles	Smooth muscles	Cardiac muscles
Other names	Striated muscles, voluntary muscles	Non-striated muscles, involuntary muscles	Heart muscles
Location	Attached to bones	In internal organs like stomach	Heart
Function	Movement	Control movement of substances inside organs, for example, food inside the stomach	Beating of the heart
Control	Voluntary (controlled by will)	Involuntary (cannot be controlled by will)	Involuntary
Speed of fatigue	Rapid	Slow	Do not get fatigued during the lifetime of an organism

Revision Zone

Fill in the blanks.

1. __________ (Epithelial/Muscular) tissues cover the entire internal and external surface of the body.
2. __________ (Skeletal/Cardiac) muscles work non-stop without getting tired.
3. Smooth muscles are __________ (voluntary/involuntary).
4. __________ (Skeletal/Smooth) muscles are attached to bones.

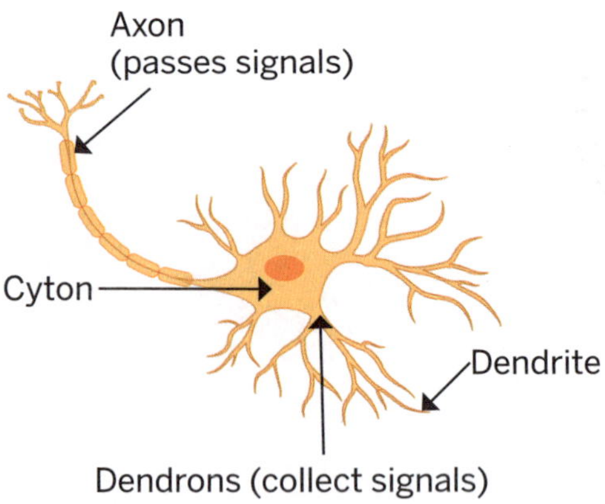

▲ Fig. 1.3 Structure of a neuron

Nervous Tissues

Nervous tissues are made up of nerve cells called **neurons**. Neurons are grouped together in the form of bundles called **nerves**. Nerves run throughout the body forming a network

Structurally, a neuron consists of the following parts.

- **Cyton**: the cell body
- **Dendrons**: finger-like projections extending from the cell body
- **Dendrites**: branches of dendrons
- **Axon**: the longest extension from the cell body

Connective Tissues

These tissues are abundantly found in the body. Their basic function is to bind one type of tissue with the other, to support organs and hold them in place. Cells in this tissue are not closely-packed. They are separated by a matrix (mesh), which they secrete.

Connective tissues can be grouped into three categories: fibrous tissues, skeletal tissues and fluid tissues.

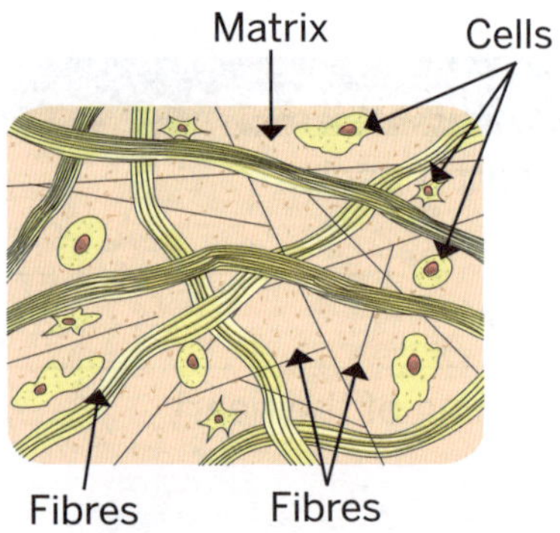

(a) Areolar tissue

(b) Adipose tissue

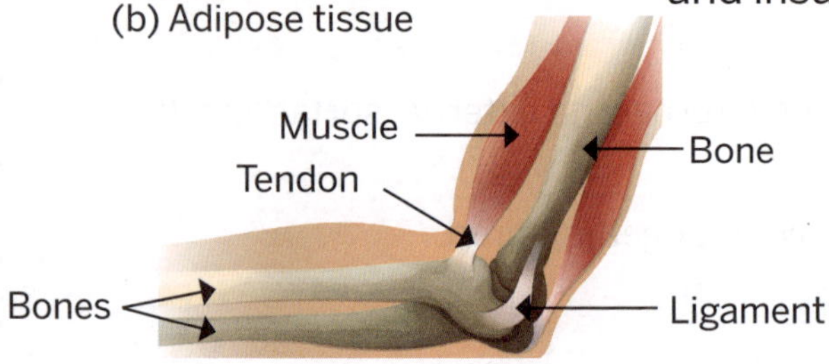

(c) Tendon and ligament

▲ Fig. 1.4 Fibrous connective tissues

Fibrous Tissues

Fibrous tissues pack and bind the organs. These can be further grouped into three types.

Areolar tissues

- These have a jelly-like matrix that encloses different kinds of cells.
- The matrix has elastic fibres that help bind skin to muscles, fill gaps between cells and hold organs in place.
- These are found in the linings of the gut, muscles, skin and other organs.

Adipose tissues

- These are connective tissues that surround the organs.
- They are also found beneath the skin and act as a cushion and insulator in the body.
- They are also called **body fat** as they store energy in the form of fat.

Tendons and ligaments

- Tendons are whitish, tough cords of thick, fibrous tissues that connect muscles to bones.
- Ligaments are bands of elastic fibres that connect different bones.

Skeletal Tissues

Skeletal connective tissues provide supportive framework to the body and can be further grouped into two types.

Bone

- It is the hardest and the most rigid connective tissue. It consists of living cells, called **osteocytes**, that are enclosed in the bone matrix.
- It is made of 7 per cent calcium and 85 per cent phosphate along with traces of sodium and magnesium.

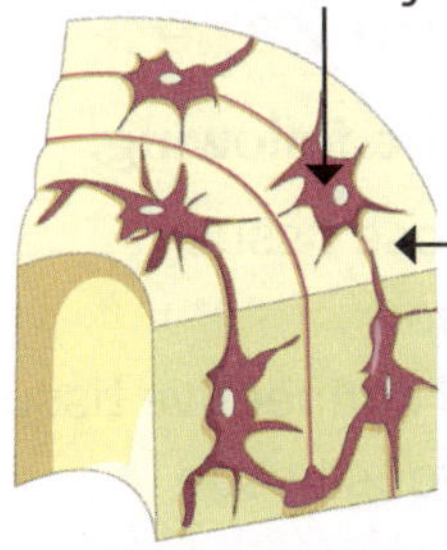

▲ Fig. 1.5 Bone tissue

Cartilage

- It is a flexible, elastic, semi-transparent but tough connective tissue.
- It is usually found at the end of the bones where it reduces friction between two bones, and in the walls of the windpipe, tip of the nose and pinna of the ear.
- The cartilage cells, called **chondrocytes**, are scattered in the matrix (chondroitin).

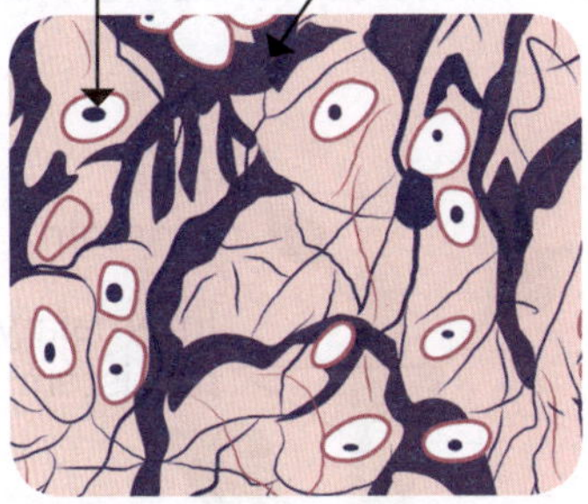

▲ Fig. 1.6 Cartilage tissue

Do You Know?

A shark's skeleton is made entirely of cartilage!

Fluid Connective Tissues

Fluid connective tissues help in the transportation of nutrients and essential substances within the body.

They can be further grouped into two types.

Blood: It consists of **plasma** (the watery matrix) in which three types of cells are found.

- **Red blood cells** (RBCs) or erythrocytes: They transport oxygen and carbon dioxide in the body.
- **White blood cells** (WBCs) or leucocytes: They fight pathogens and other foreign substances.
- **Platelets** or thrombocytes: They help in clotting of blood.

Lymph: It is a fluid that is present around body cells. It is also called **blood without RBCs**. Lymph fluids protect the body against any infection.

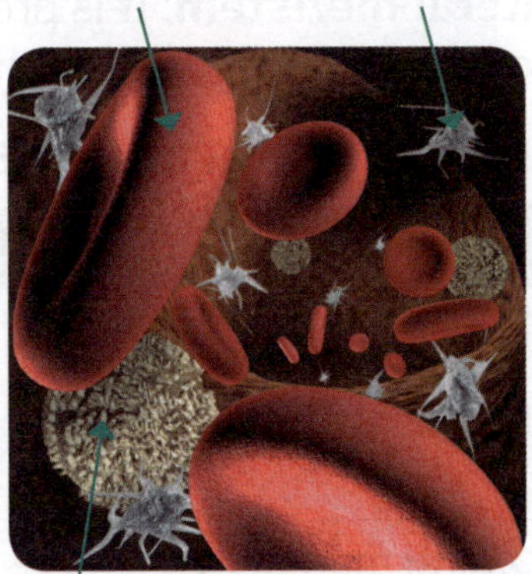

▲ Fig. 1.7 Blood cells

Activity 1

Aim: To observe the slides of animal tissues

Procedure: Ask your teacher to provide some permanent slides of animal tissues. Focus these under a microscope with your teacher's help and observe. Draw what you see in your notebook and write two features of each type of tissue that you see.

Revision Zone

Match the following.

1.	Adipose tissue	a.	Connects muscle to bone
2.	Tendon	b.	Store fat
3.	Fluid connective tissue	c.	Neuron
4.	Nervous tissue	d.	Lymph

Plant Tissues

Plant tissues can be divided into two categories: meristematic tissues and permanent tissues.

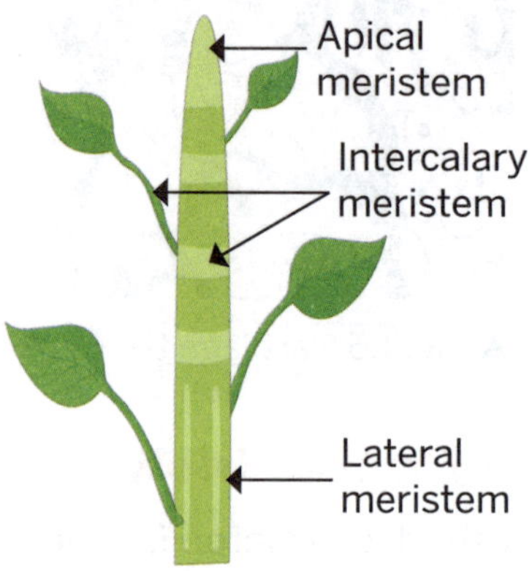

▲ Fig. 1.8 Meristematic tissues

Meristematic Tissues

- Cells are small and thin-walled with large nuclei, and almost no vacuoles and intercellular space. Cells divide actively giving rise to more cells.
- Function of meristematic tissue is to bring about growth.

Meristematic tissue is of three types.

Apical meristem: It is present at the tip of the growing parts like root tip, and tip of the stem and branches. It causes growth at the root and shoot tips.

Intercalary meristem: It is found in places where the stem is attached with the leaves and at the bases of the leaves. It causes an increase in the length of the stem.

Lateral meristem: It is present between water-conducting and food-conducting tissues. It causes an increase in the thickness of the stem.

Table 1.2 Types of meristematic tissues

Type	Location	Function
Apical meristem	Root and shoot tips	Growth
Intercalary meristem	Bases of leaves and place of attachment of stem and leaves	Increases length of the stem
Lateral meristem	Between water-conducting and food-conducting tissues	Increases thickness of the stem

Permanent Tissues

These tissues form the bulk of the plant body. The cells do not grow or divide after reaching a certain size. Permanent tissues are of two types: simple permanent tissues and complex permanent tissues.

Simple Permanent Tissues

Based on their functions, simple permanent tissues can be grouped into two types: protective tissues and supporting tissues.

Protective Tissues

- The outer protective layers of the plant are commonly known as **epidermis**. They are composed of closely-packed cells without intercellular spaces.
- Tissues in the outer walls of the plant are usually thickened and covered with wax and cuticle.
- Epidermal cells in the leaves have openings called **stomata**, which are surrounded by **guard cells**. The opening and closing of stomata is regulated by the guard cells.

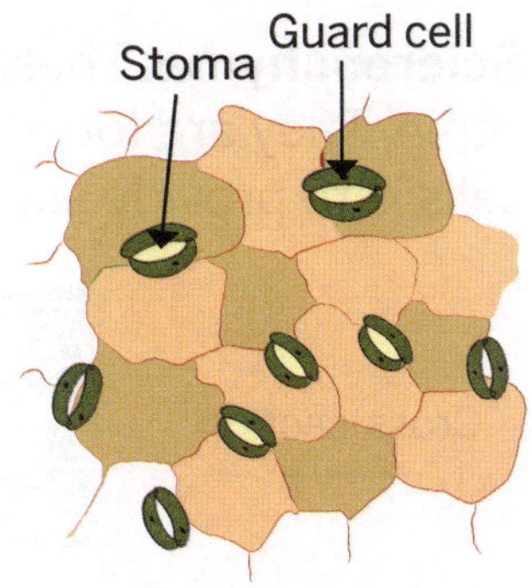

▲ Fig. 1.9 Epidermis

Activity 2

Aim: To observe the stomata in a leaf of a balsam plant

Materials required: Fresh balsam leaf, distilled water, glycerine, safranin stain, glass plate, slide, cover slip, and microscope

Procedure:

1. Take a fresh balsam leaf, fold it carefully and tear along the lower side of the leaf.
2. A colourless narrow border (epidermis) found along the torn edge should be carefully pulled out.
3. Place the epidermis in a glass plate containing distilled water.
4. Transfer the epidermis onto a glass slide and add a drop of safranin solution. Leave it for 30–60 seconds to stain the peel.
5. Remove excess stain by rinsing it with distilled water.
6. Add a few drops of glycerine and cover it with a cover slip.

Observation: Draw what you see in your notebook. Compare this with the diagram of the epidermis and stomata given above.

Supporting Tissues

These tissues constitute the primary plant body or the bulk of the plant. These tissues can be further grouped into three types.

- **Parenchyma**: This is found in all soft parts of the plant. Cells are round to oval in shape with thin, flexible cell walls and a large vacuole with ample intercellular space. These cells help in the storage of food and water. The intercellular space aids in the exchange of gases in the cells of the plant.
- **Collenchyma**: These have elongated cells that are thicker at the corners and are made of substances called **cellulose** and **pectin**. They are found under the epidermis of the plant. These cells may sometimes contain chloroplasts. These cells provide structural support and elasticity to the stem and leaves of the plant.

- **Sclerenchyma**: These are dead cells with a very thick cell wall made of cellulose and lignin. They are found in the veins and stems of the plant. The function of sclerenchyma cells is to provide support and rigidity.

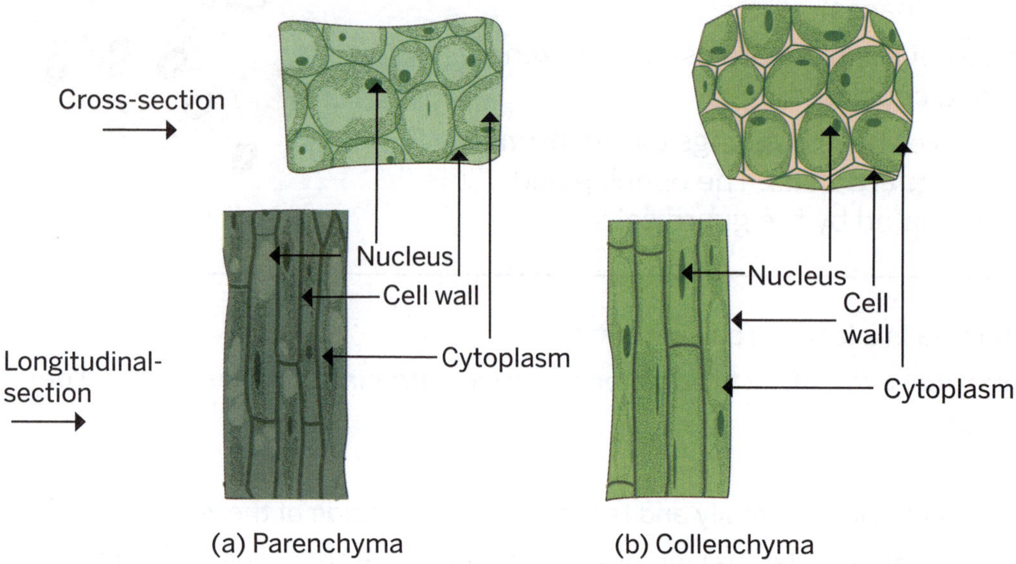

▲ Fig. 1.10 Supporting tissues

Activity 3

Aim: To view the slides of plant tissues

Procedure: Ask your teacher to give you some permanent slides of plant tissues. Focus these under a microscope with your teacher's help and observe.

Observation: Draw what you see in your notebook and write two characteristics of each tissue.

Revision Zone

Fill in the blank portions of the given table.

Category	Parenchyma	Collenchyma	Sclerenchyma
Location	Stem, root, leaves, flowers, widely distributed in fruits		
Shape of cells		Cells are living; circular, oval or polygonal with thickened corners of walls	Cells are dead; long, narrow, pointed; uniformly thick walls
Arrangement of cells	Loosely arranged with intercellular spaces		Intercellular spaces are absent
Functions	Stores and assimilates food; provides mechanical support; stores waste products like tannin gum, resins		

Complex Permanent Tissues

These tissues are made up of two or more different types of specialized cells that carry out a single specific function. They are also called **conducting tissues** as their primary function is to conduct materials in the plant body.

Based on their functions, complex permanent tissues can be grouped into xylem tissues and phloem tissues. Xylem and phloem tissues together are called **vascular tissues**.

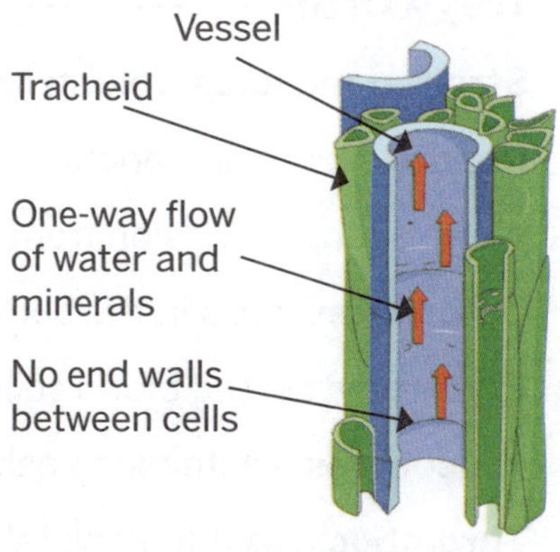

(a) Xylem

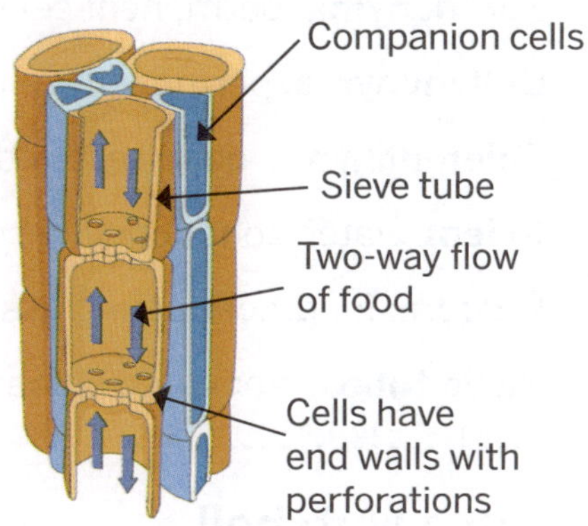

(b) Phloem

▲ Fig. 1.11 Complex permanent tissues

Xylem Tissues

- Xylem is a bundle of cells that are often dead.
- They have thick cell walls and are placed end to end, one above the other in the form of a pipeline.
- Xylem is composed of different types of cells called vessels and tracheids. It also contains fibres and parenchyma.
- The function of xylem tissues is to transport water and minerals from the roots to the other parts of the plant.

Phloem Tissues

- Phloem is a bundle of living cells with narrow, elongated and thin cell walls.
- Phloem is composed of sieve tubes and companion cells. It also contains fibres and parenchyma.
- Main functions of phloem tissues include transportation of food prepared in the leaves to various plant parts.

Activity 4

Aim: To infer that transportation of water and minerals takes place through the xylem

Materials required: Glass beaker, water, a plant twig, stain/ink, cover slip, blade, slide and microscope

Procedure: Fill a glass beaker three-fourth with water. Place a plant twig in the beaker. Add a few drops of ink to the beaker and leave it for some time. Cut a thin section of the plant stem from the set-up with the help of a blade. Transfer the section to a clean glass slide. Place a cover slip and focus the slide under the microscope with the help of your teacher.

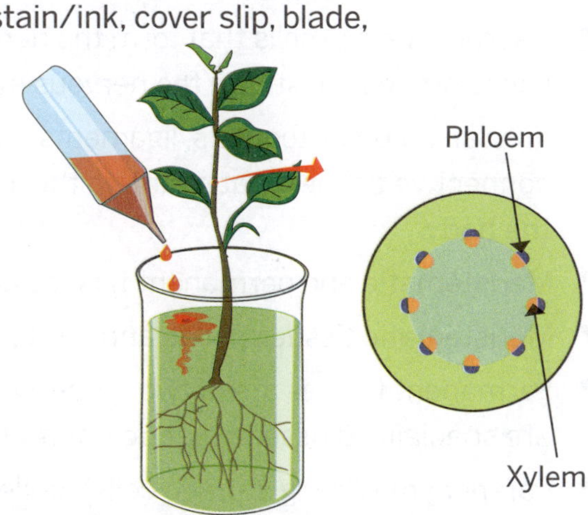

Observation: Tubes coloured with the colour of the ink are visible towards the centre of the section.

Conclusion: Water is transported from the roots to other parts of the plant body through xylem and when a section of the stem is viewed under the microscope, a few parts of the tissues in the vascular bundles appear coloured. These are the xylem tissues.

Keywords

Striated muscles: voluntary muscles with alternate dark and light bands

Dendrites: small branches of dendrons in a neuron that collect signals

Axon: a long extension from the cell body in a neuron that transmits information

Osteocytes: cells in the bone tissue matrix

Erythrocytes: red blood cells

Leucocytes: white blood cells

Thrombocytes: blood platelets

Meristematic cells: cells that continuously divide and grow

Parenchyma: permanent cells with thin cell walls

Collenchyma: permanent cells with cell walls with thickened corners

Sclerenchyma: dead cells with thickened cell walls

Xylem: water-conducting tissues in plants

Phloem: food-conducting tissues in plants

Sieve tubes: elongated phloem cells without nucleus

In a Nutshell

- Epithelial tissues, connective tissues, muscular tissues and nervous tissues are the four basic tissues found in animals.
- Epithelial tissues cover the outer layers of the organs. These are of three types: squamous, columnar and cuboidal.
- Muscular tissues help in movement. Depending upon their location in the body, they can be grouped into three types: cardiac, skeletal and smooth.
- Neurons are the cells that form the nervous system. The brain, spinal cord, nerves and the sense organs constitute the nervous system.
- Areolar, adipose, tendons, ligaments, bones, cartilage, blood and lymph are the basic connective tissues that maintain the interconnection between the different organs of the body.
- Meristematic and permanent tissues are the two types of plant tissues.
- Meristematic tissues divide and multiply, thus, increasing the length and girth of the plant.
- Permanent tissues are of two types: simple permanent and complex permanent. These are specialized tissues that do not multiply actively.
- Parenchyma (living storage cells), collenchyma (living structural support cells) and sclerenchyma (dead structural support cells) are simple permanent tissues.
- Xylem (water-conducting tissues) and phloem (food-conducting tissues) are complex permanent tissues.

Mind Map

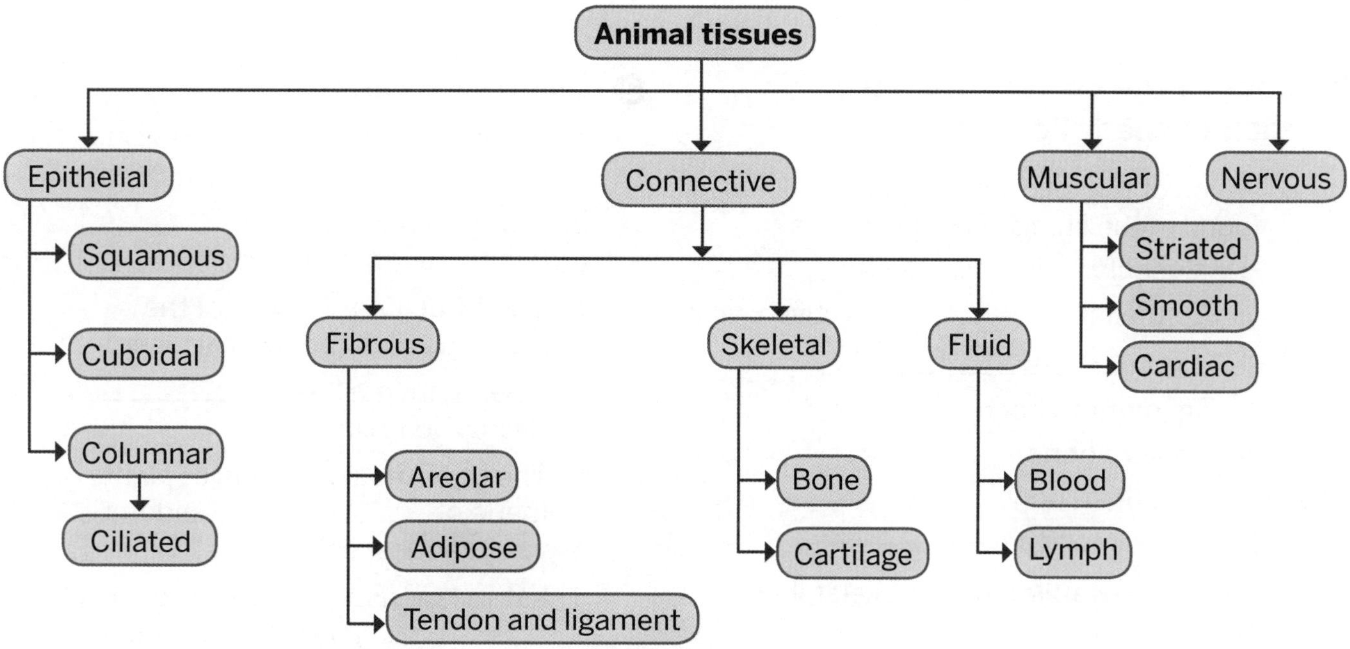

Animal tissues
Epithelial
Squamous
Cuboidal
Columnar
Ciliated
Connective
Fibrous
Areolar
Adipose
Tendon and ligament
Skeletal
Bone
Cartilage
Fluid
Blood
Lymph
Muscular
Striated
Smooth
Cardiac
Nervous

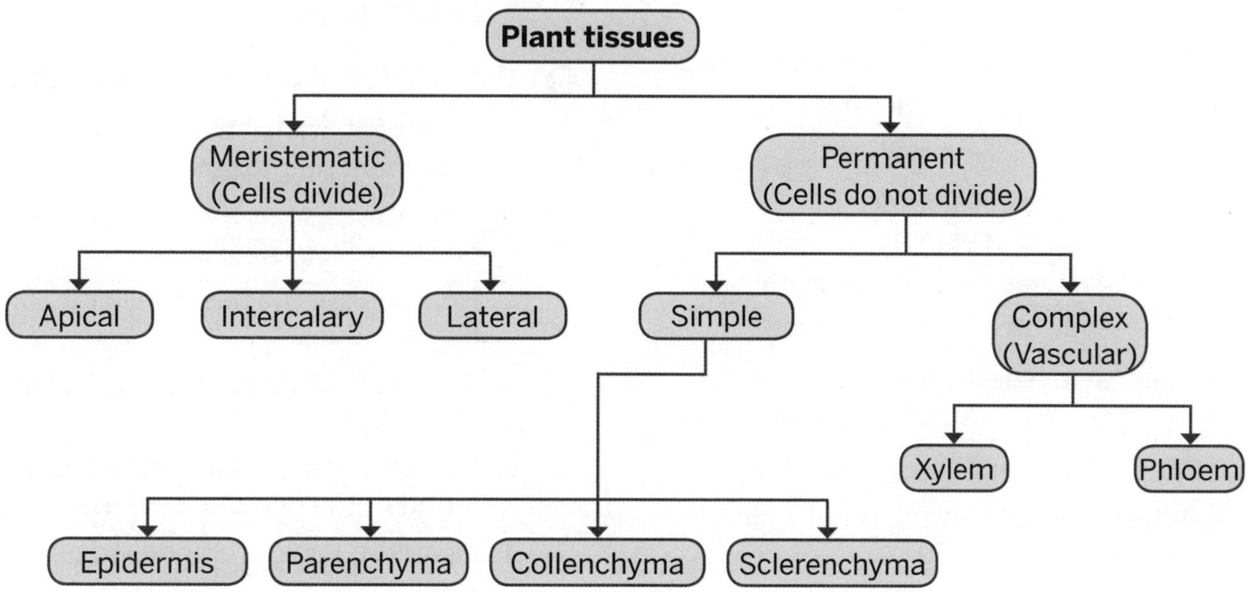

Plant tissues
Meristematic (Cells divide)
Apical
Intercalary
Lateral
Permanent (Cells do not divide)
Simple
Epidermis
Parenchyma
Collenchyma
Sclerenchyma
Complex (Vascular)
Xylem
Phloem

Exercise

1. Choose the correct answer for each of the following.

a. Which of the following tissues are found in the lining of blood vessels?
   i. Muscular ii. Nervous
   iii. Epithelial iv. Connective

b. Tendon connects ___________.
   i. ligament to bone
   ii. bone to bone
   iii. muscle to bone
   iv. muscle to ligament

c. Which of the following is a skeletal connective tissue?
   i. Blood ii. Cartilage
   iii. Adipose iv. Nerve

d. Blood is a ___________ connective tissue.
   i. fibrous ii. hard
   iii. fluid iv. soft

e. Neurons are cells of the ___________ system.
   i. digestive ii. skeletal
   iii. respiratory iv. nervous

f. Adipose tissue stores ___________.
   i. fats ii. carbohydrates
   iii. proteins iv. vitamins

g. Which of the following is not a simple permanent tissue?
   i. Parenchyma ii. Collenchyma
   iii. Sclerenchyma iv. Xylem

h. Cells in the apical meristem ___________.
   i. do not divide ii. divide actively
   iii. are dead iv. none of these

i. Which of the following plant tissues conducts food?
   i. Parenchyma ii. Phloem
   iii. Collenchyma iv. Xylem

2. Fill in the blanks.

a. Areolar connective tissue has a ___________ (fluid/fibrous) matrix.

b. Lymph is blood minus ___________ (white/red) blood cells.

c. Chondrocytes are cells of the ___________ (bones/cartilage).

d. Sclerenchyma has ___________ (living/dead) cells.

e. The outermost covering of plants is made of ___________ (epidermis/vascular tissues).

f. Lateral meristem causes growth in ___________ (length/thickness).

g. Sieve tubes are found in ___________ (xylem/phloem) tissues.

3. Write T for True and F for False.

a. Cells of epithelial tissues have a basement membrane.

b. Smooth muscles are striated and can be controlled by will.

c. Neurons are the basic cell units of nerve tissues.

d. Cardiac muscles are also called smooth muscles.

e. Cartilage is a connective tissue usually found at the end of the bones.

f. Ligament joins two bones together.

g. Fluid connective tissues help in the transportation of nutrients and essential substances within the body.

h. Parenchyma is a type of simple permanent tissue.

i. Sclerenchyma has elongated cells that are thick at the corners.

❹ Answer the following questions in brief.

a. Define tissues.

b. What are the three types of epithelial tissues?

c. What is areolar tissue?

d. What are tendons and ligaments?

e. What are cardiac muscles?

f. What are osteocytes?

g. Name the different types of fibrous connective tissues.

h. Which tissue causes growth in plants?

i. What is epidermis in plants?

j. Write a note on meristematic tissues.

❺ Answer the following questions in detail.

a. Write a note on epithelial tissue.

b. What are muscular tissues? Explain the three types of muscular tissues.

c. Write a note on fibrous connective tissue.

d. Write a note on nerve tissues. Describe the structure of a neuron with the help of a diagram.

e. Write a short note on fluid connective tissues.

f. What are the different types of simple permanent tissues in plants?

g. Explain the complex permanent tissues of plants.

h. Describe the vascular tissues found in plants.

❻ Differentiate between the following.

a. Meristematic and permanent tissues

b. Xylem and phloem

c. Collenchyma and sclerenchyma

d. Parenchyma and collenchyma

e. Ligament and tendon

f. Skeletal muscles and smooth muscles

g. Areolar tissue and adipose tissue

h. Bone and cartilage

❼ In the Library

Find out how many different layers are there in the human integumentary system.

❽ Thinking Beyond

With advancements in technology, scientists have been able to generate tissues under artificial conditions in laboratories. This technique is called tissue culture.

Find out more about the process, its merits and demerits.

❾ Project

Do an activity to observe the conduction of water by stem.

Materials required: Two long twigs of white chrysanthemum or white carnation with a flower on each, food dyes or ink, two beakers and water

Procedure:

1. Take equal volume of water in the beakers. Mark them A and B.
2. Add ink to the water in beaker B. You can also add food dyes instead of ink.
3. Place one twig in each beaker and leave the set-up for 24 hours.

Observation: Observe the colour of the flower on each twig after 24 hours.

Discuss your observations in class. What do you infer from the observation?

Worksheet

Subject Integration

1 Complete the flowchart of different types of tissues found in the animals.

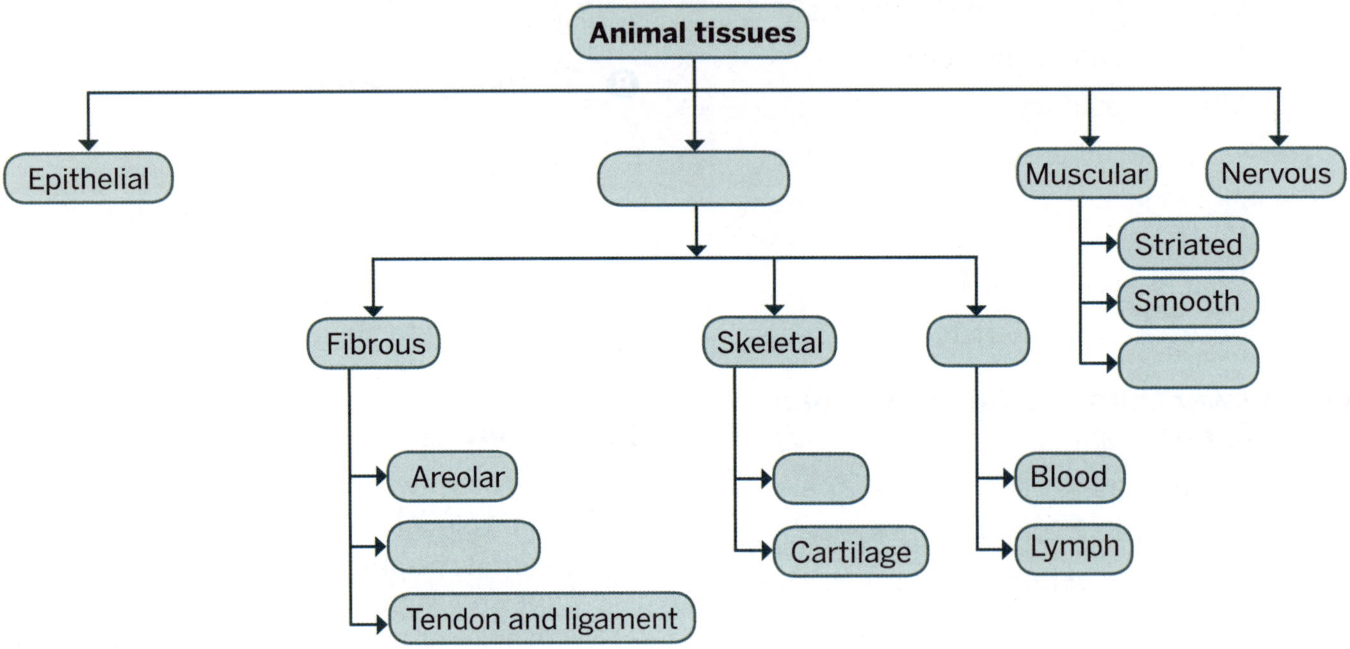

2 In the diagram of the plant given below, label the parts where the following will be found:

(a) Apical meristem (b) Intercalary meristem (c) Lateral meristem

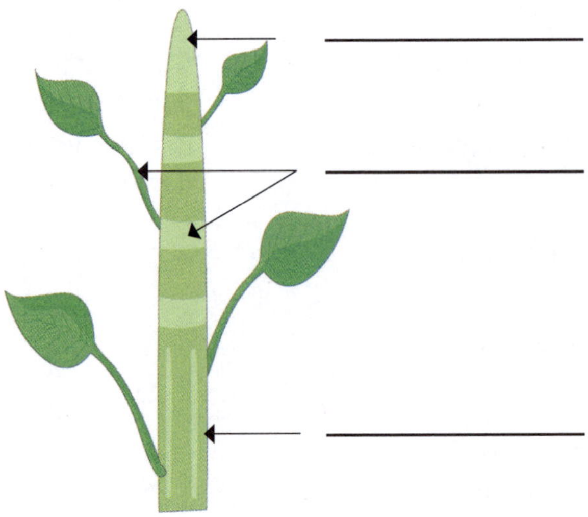

Kingdom Classification

2

What I shall learn

- Meaning of classification
- Advantages of classifying living things
- Two-kingdom classification
- Five-kingdom classification
- General plan of classification
- Scientific names of some plants and animals

Science in Context

Taxonomy is the branch of biology that systematically classifies living things based on similarities in structure, origin, etc. Scientists who study taxonomy are called **taxonomists**.

Introduction

The term **classification** means to sort or categorize things into groups. In our daily lives, we often come across situations where things have been sorted into groups. For example, in a supermarket, food items are sorted into various categories like vegetables, fruits, spices and packaged foods. This makes it convenient to locate the food item of our choice. However, imagine the confusion and inconvenience it would cause if all the food items were mixed and there were no separate shelves for different categories.

There are around 30 million types of living organisms on Earth. It would be impossible to locate and study these without sorting them first into groups. Scientists realized this need a long time ago and started categorizing organisms under separate groups based on similar characteristics, to make it easy to study them.

Biological Classification

Classifying living organisms into different groups and subgroups based on similarities in their characteristics is called **biological classification**.

The advantages of classifying living things are:

- Classification makes it easy to identify and study living organisms on Earth.
- Classification helps in identifying a new organism and placing it in a particular group.
- It helps in getting an overview of the characteristics of a particular group of organisms, so that one does not need to memorize the characteristics of each type of organism in that group.
- It gives a clear idea about the evolution of organisms from simple forms to more complex ones.
- It establishes the relationship between different living things.

Know the Scientist

Aristotle (384 BC–322 BC) was a philosopher and scientist from ancient Greece. He made the first attempt to classify living things. He is considered the father of biology.

Know the Scientist

Carolus Linnaeus (1707–1778) was a Swedish botanist, physician and zoologist who laid the foundation for scientifically naming biologically classified organisms. He is also considered the father of modern taxonomy.

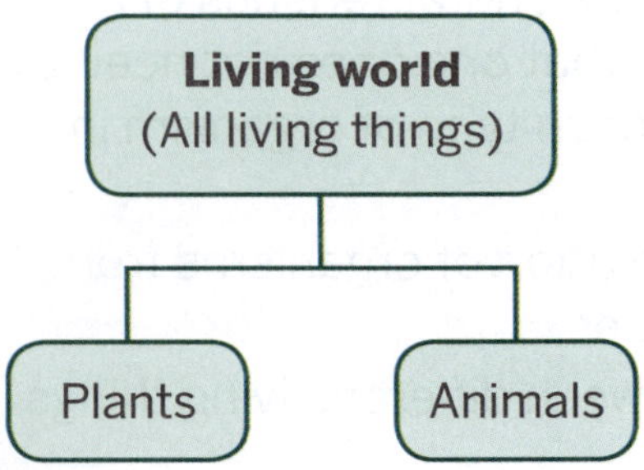

Different Systems of Classification

Living things are classified based on their habits, habitats, mode of reproduction and other features.

Aristotle, a Greek philosopher, was the first to classify animals based on simple visible characteristics like the type of body covering (hard or soft), the mode of reproduction (laying eggs or giving birth to young ones) and the presence or absence of red-coloured blood.

Theophrastus, a follower and successor of Aristotle, classified plants on the basis of size into herbs, shrubs, under shrubs and trees.

The above-mentioned method of classification based on visible characteristics had some major drawbacks. Two very different organisms could be put in the same group; for example, based on the presence of wings, birds and insects can be categorized under the same group although they are very different in other characteristics. Similarly, rose plants and ferns can be categorized under the same group based on size, although they are very different otherwise.

Two-kingdom Classification

To overcome these drawbacks, in the year 1758, a Swedish botanist named Carolus Linnaeus proposed a more scientific method of classification. He classified living organisms into two kingdoms: Kingdom Plantae and Kingdom Animalia.

Kingdom Plantae

It includes organisms that prepare their own food, but are stationary, that is, they cannot move around.

Kingdom Animalia

It includes organisms that cannot prepare their own food, but can move around.

Linnaeus further classified each kingdom into smaller groups based on similar characteristics. Each group was further divided into subgroups and so on. This way, several taxonomic ranks were developed. The lowest rank had organisms with most features in common, that is, they were the most closely-related.

Five-kingdom Classification

Microorganisms were discovered after the invention of the microscope. With advances in technology, powerful microscopes were built, which gave a better understanding of the cell structure of microorganisms. Microorganisms were found to have characteristics that made them unsuitable to be grouped under the plant or the animal kingdom. Further observations and discoveries led to an increased knowledge about the evolution and structures of organisms. As a result, the two-kingdom classification began to be considered inadequate to group all these organisms.

In 1969, RH Whittaker proposed the **five-kingdom classification** system to cater to the necessity of classifying all the known organisms.

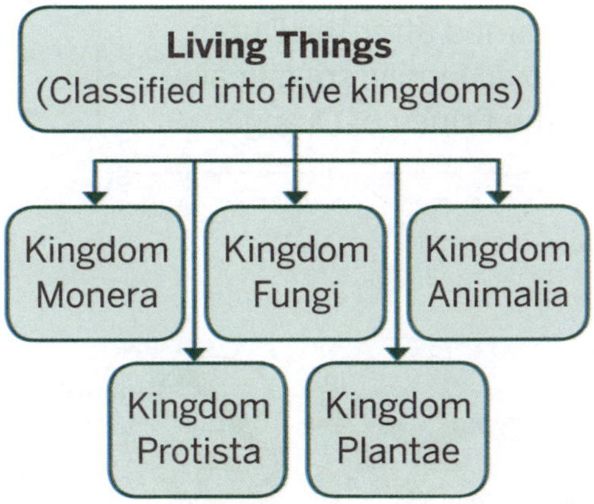

Let us look at the characteristics of the organisms grouped under each kingdom.

Kingdom Monera

- They are unicellular, that is, the entire body is made up of a single cell.
- The cells lack a well-defined nucleus. The genetic material in the cell lies in the cytoplasm.
- Their cells have a **cell wall** as an outer covering.
- Some organisms in this kingdom are **autotrophic**, that is, they can prepare their own food, for example, blue-green algae, while others are **heterotrophic**, that is, they depend on other sources for food, for example, *E. Coli*.
- Bacteria are grouped under this kingdom and have different shapes. Some are long and rod-like (bacilli), some are spherical (cocci), some are spiral (spirilla) and some are comma-shaped (vibrio).
- Some monerans have whip-like structures called **flagella**, which help them to move. Others are immotile.

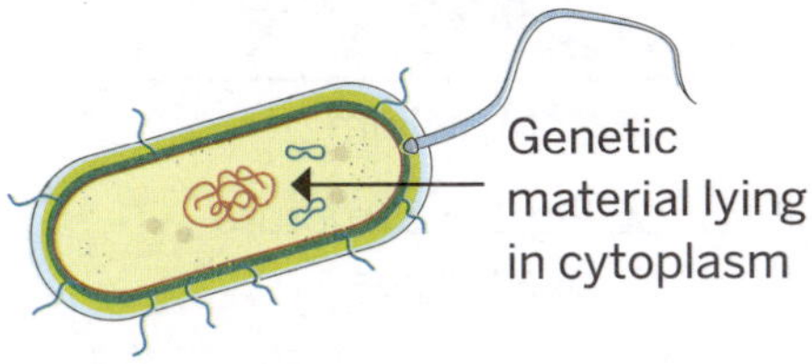

▲ Fig. 2.1 Bacteria lack a well-defined nucleus

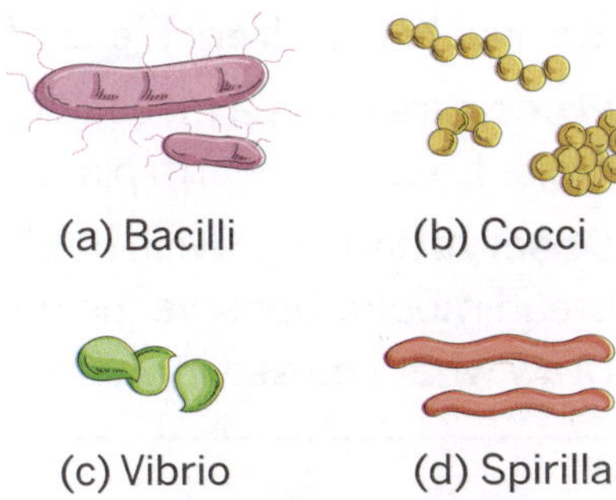

▲ Fig. 2.2 Different shapes of bacteria

Kingdom Protista

- They are unicellular.
- The genetic material of the cell is found inside a well-defined nucleus with a nuclear membrane.
- A few organisms are autotrophic, for example, diatoms and *Euglena*, while some are heterotrophic, for example, *Paramoecium* and *Amoeba*.
- They move with the help of special structures. Some of the special structures are:
  cilia – hair-like structures (for example, in *Paramoecium*)
  flagella (singular: flagellum) – a whip-like structure (for example, in *Trypanosoma*)
  pseudopodia – false limbs (for example in *Amoeba*)

▲ Fig. 2.3 *Paramoecium*

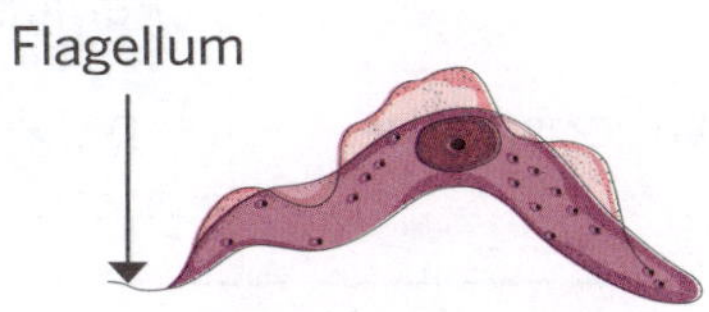

▲ Fig. 2.4 *Trypanosoma*

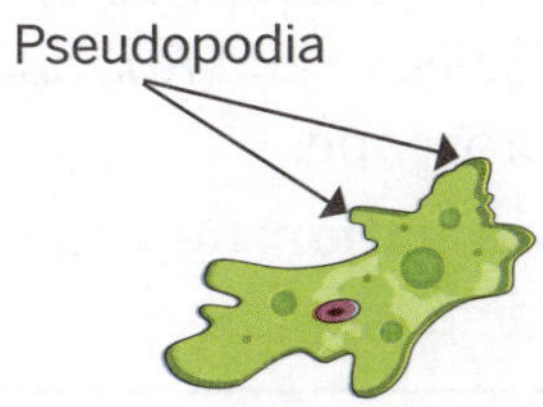

▲ Fig. 2.5 *Amoeba*

Do You Know?

A new fungus was discovered in 2013 in Netherlands. It is called Orange Penicillium and named after the Dutch royal family, specifically the Prince of Orange.

Kingdom Fungi

- Fungi are **non-green** organisms with cells having a well-defined nucleus. Some examples are moulds, mushrooms and yeast.
- Except yeast, all other fungi are multicellular.
- Their cells have a **cell wall** made of a substance called **chitin**.
- Fungi depend on other organisms for food (heterotrophs).
- The body of a multicellular fungus is known as **mycelium**, which is made up of thread-like structures known as **hyphae**. Examples of fungi are *Mucor*, *Penicillium* and *Rhizopus*.

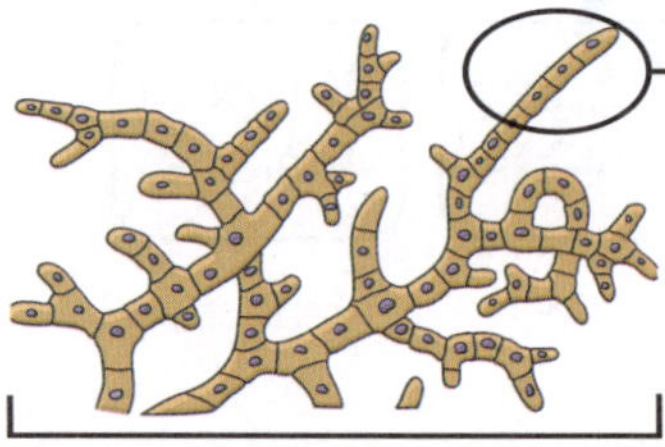

▲ Fig. 2.6 Structure of a fungus

▲ Fig. 2.7 *Penicillium*

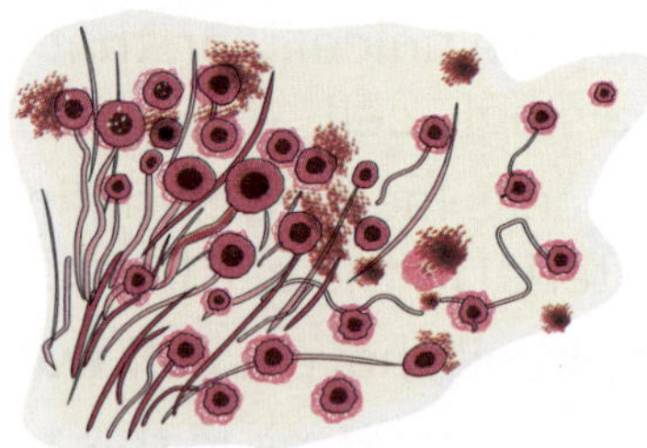

▲ Fig. 2.8 *Rhizopus*

Activity 1

Aim: To observe a bread mould

Materials required: Piece of bread, glass of water and compound microscope

Procedure: Take a piece of bread and make it moist with a small amount of water. Keep this moist bread in a warm place undisturbed for two to three days.

Observation: A greyish or blackish cotton-like mass will appear on the bread. This is called bread mould. Observe the mould under a microscope with the help of your teacher.
Draw what you see in your notebook.

Activity 2

Aim: To observe the structure of different fungi

Materials required: Compound microscope, permanent slides of *Mucor*, yeast, *Penicillium* and *Rhizopus* (to be provided by the teacher)

Procedure: With the help of your teacher, observe the permanent slides of *Mucor*, yeast, *Penicillium* and *Rhizopus* under a compound microscope.

Observation: Record your observations in the given table.

Fungus	Multicellular/ Unicellular	Presence of hyphae (Yes or No)
Mucor		
Yeast		
Penicillium		
Rhizopus		

Kingdom Plantae

- They are **multicellular** and **autotrophic** organisms.
- All organisms within this kingdom have the pigment called **chlorophyll** and prepare their own food.
- They have a **cell wall** made of **cellulose**.
- The Kingdom Plantae is subdivided into various classes—thallophyta, bryophyta, pteridophyta, gymnosperms and angiosperms. We will discuss more about them in the next chapter.

All plants belong to Kingdom Plantae.

Greenathon

Gift a plant for every celebration. This way, we can contribute to nature and celebrate life.

Kingdom Animalia

- They are **multicellular** and heterotrophic organisms.
- They do not have a cell wall.
- The Kingdom Animalia is further divided into vertebrates and invertebrates.

All animals, including human beings, belong to Kingdom Animalia.

Challenge Yourself

You have studied about microorganisms called viruses. They have not been included in any kingdom. Find out why.

Revision Zone

Match the following.

1. Kingdom Plantae	a. *Amoeba*
2. Kingdom Fungi	b. Human being
3. Kingdom Protista	c. Mint plant
4. Kingdom Animalia	d. *Rhizopus*
5. Kingdom Monera	e. Bacteria

General Plan of Classification

A scientifically classified group is known as a **rank** (plural: ranks) **or taxon** (plural: taxa). The hierarchy of groups is as follows:

Kingdom

This is the highest rank. As discussed earlier, Carolus Linnaeus had divided the living world into two kingdoms: plant and animal kingdom. However, modern science follows the five-kingdom classification system given by Whittaker.

Phylum/Division

Each kingdom is further divided into many phyla (singular: phylum) based on similarities. For example, the plant kingdom is divided into two phyla, namely, flowering and non-flowering plants.

Class

Organisms in a Phylum are grouped into various classes. For example, animals that give birth to young ones and suckle them with milk are grouped under the class Mammalia. Flowering plants are divided into two classes called monocotyledons and dicotyledons based on the number of cotyledons (seed leaves) their seeds contain.

Order

Each class is divided into subgroups known as orders. For example, carnivorous animals are grouped under the order Carnivora. Plants that yield fibres are grouped under the order Malvales.

> **Remember**
>
> An easy way to remember these taxonomic hierarchies is to remember this mnemonic:
>
> **K**eep **P**ots **C**lean **O**r **F**amily **G**ets **S**ick
>
> The bold letters denote the first letter of each taxonomic rank.
>
> K: Kingdom; P: Phylum; C: Class; O: Order; F: Family; G: Genus; S: Species

Family

Under each order of animals and plants, there are many families. For example, cats are grouped under the family Felidae. Plants that bear rose-like flowers are grouped under the family Rosaceae.

Genus

The animals and plants that belong to a family are divided into genera (singular: genus). For example, although tiger, lion and cat belong to the same family, they belong to different genera. Tigers and lions belong to the genus Panthera while cats belong to the genus Felis. The plant family Rosaceae has many genera. One among them is called Prunus; it includes cherries and almonds.

Species

The individual members of a genus that are capable of interbreeding or producing offsprings are known as **species** (plural: species). The species is the lowest ranked category in the hierarchy of classification and contains two parts in its name. The first part is the name of the genus, written with the first letter in capital, and the second part is the name of the organism, written in small letters. This system of naming organisms is called the **binomial system of nomenclature**. The names of the genus and species are always printed in italics, but when they are handwritten, they are underlined separately. For example, *Panthera tigris* (tiger) or *P. tigris*.

Table 2.1 Scientific names of animals and plants

Some scientific names of animals and plants along with their taxonomical classification	
Kingdom: Animalia (Animals)	Kingdom: Animalia (Animals)
Phylum: Chordata (Vertebrate)	Phylum: Chordata (Vertebrate)
Class: Mammalia (Mammal)	Class: Mammalia (Mammal)
Order: Carnivora (Carnivore)	Order: Primates (Primate)
Family: Felidae (Cat)	Family: Hominidae (Great ape)
Genus: Panthera	Genus: Homo
Species: *Panthera tigris* (Tiger) 	Species: *Homo sapiens* (Human being) 

Kingdom: Plantae (Plants)
Phylum: Angiosperms
Class: Eudicots
Order: Malvales
Family: Malvaceae
Genus: Hibiscus
Species: *Hibiscus rosa-sinensis* (Hibiscus plant)

Kingdom: Plantae (Plants)
Phylum: Gymnosperms
Class: Cycadopsida
Order: Cycadales
Family: Cycadaceae
Genus: Cycas
Species: *Cycas taitungensis* (Cycas plant)

Revision Zone

Fill in the blanks.

1. A scientifically classified group is known as ________.
2. ________ is the highest rank in taxonomy.
3. Members of a genus capable of interbreeding or producing offspring are called ________.
4. Cats are grouped under the family ________.
5. The scientific name of hibiscus plant is ________.

Keywords

Classification: grouping of living things based on common characteristics

Taxonomy: the branch of biology that systematically classifies living things

Kingdom: the largest group or division of classification

Taxon: each unit of classification is also known as rank or taxon

Genus: group of living things that have common characteristics

Species: individual members of the group genus that can interbreed to produce offspring

In a Nutshell

- Classifying living organisms into different groups and subgroups based on similarities in their characteristics is called biological classification.
- Earlier, living things were classified into two groups, animals and plants, by Carolus Linnaeus.
- RH Whittaker proposed the five-kingdom classification to cater to the need for classification of all known organisms.
- The modern classification system includes kingdoms—Monera, Protista, Fungi, Animalia and Plantae.
- The various taxonomical ranks (highest to lowest) are Kingdom, Phylum, Class, Order, Family, Genus and Species.

Exercise

1. Choose the correct answer for each of the following.

a. Carolus Linnaeus divided living things into ________ kingdoms.
   i. three ii. five
   iii. two iv. four

b. Classification based on simple visible characteristics was first done by
   i. Linnaeus ii. Aristotle
   iii. Whittaker iv. Theophrastus

c. What is true about bacteria?
   i. They do not have a well-defined nucleus.
   ii. They belong to Kingdom Protista.
   iii. The cell wall is made of chitin.
   iv. They are multicellular.

d. *Paramoecium* belongs to Kingdom ________.
   i. Monera ii. Animalia
   iii. Fungi iv. Protista

e. Body of a multicellular fungi is known as
   i. Mycelium ii. Pseudopodia
   iii. Hyphae iv. Cilia

f. Which of these kingdoms has multicellular, autotrophic organisms with cell walls?
   i. Animalia ii. Fungi
   iii. Plantae iv. Protista

g. Which of these contains two parts in its name?
   i. Kingdom ii. Species
   iii. Phylum iv. Family

h. Which of these is the highest rank of classification?
   i. Order ii. Class
   iii. Family iv. Kingdom

i. The lowest taxonomical rank is
   i. genus ii. Phylum
   iii. species iv. group

2. Fill in the blanks.

a. ______ (Aristotle/Carolus Linnaeus) gave the two-kingdom classification.

b. The five-kingdom classification was proposed by ______ (RH Whittaker/ Carolus Linnaeus).

c. Organisms of Kingdom Monera have cells ______ (with/without) a well-defined nucleus.

d. *Amoeba* moves with the help of ______ (cilia/pseudopodia).

e. In Kingdom Plantae, the cell wall is made of ______ (chitin/cellulose).

f. Special structures for movement in *Paramoecium* are called ______ (flagella/cilia).

g. Organisms of Kingdom Fungi have cell walls made of ______ (cellulose/chitin).

h. Living things that belong to a particular kingdom are further divided into ______ (classes/phyla).

3. Write T for True and F for False.

a. Each class is further grouped into different orders.

b. Kingdom is the smallest rank of taxonomy.

c. Organisms of Kingdom Plantae are heterotrophic.

d. Kingdom Protista has unicellular organisms that lack a well-defined nucleus.

e. *Homo sapiens* is the scientific name of cats.

f. Plants that bear rose-like flowers are grouped under the family Rosaceae.

g. The group of animals that gives birth to young ones is grouped under Mammalia.

4 Differentiate between the following.

a. Two-kingdom and five-kingdom classifications
b. Kingdom Monera and Kingdom Protista
c. Genus and species
d. Kingdom and Phylum

5 Answer the following questions in brief.

a. List the various structures that help in locomotion in organisms of Kingdom Protista.

b. Write any two features of Kingdom Plantae.

c. Name any two kingdoms that consist of unicellular organisms.

d. What is taxonomy?

e. Name the five kingdoms classified by RH Whittaker.

f. Name the ranks of classification.

g. The scientific name of an organism contains two parts. What do these parts represent?

h. Name any three organisms that belong to Kingdom Fungi.

6 Answer the following questions in detail.

a. What is classification? Give the advantages of classifying living things.

b. List the characteristic features of Kingdom Fungi.

c. List the characteristic features of Kingdom Animalia.

d. Explain the general plan of classification.

e. Write a note on classification based on simple visible characteristics. What are its drawbacks?

f. Write a note on the five-kingdom classification.

g. Write a note on the two-kingdom classification.

h. Explain the binomial system of nomenclature. Also, give some examples.

7 Think and answer.

a. What could be the advantage of using scientific names for organisms instead of common or popular names?

(Hint: Scientific names are the key to identifying organisms.)

b. Why are saprophytes important in an ecosystem?

(Hint: Saprophytes live on dead and decaying matter.)

8 Project

Make a list of ten animals with their common names. Find out their scientific names. Collect their pictures and paste them in your scrapbook. Below every picture, write their common and scientific names.

9 In the Library

Find out the scientific names of any ten plants that you know by referring to library books.

10 In the Laboratory

Observe slides of some unicellular microscopic organisms that use different types of structures for locomotion like pseudopodia, flagella and cilia.

11 Thinking Beyond

Find out how scientific classification of organisms helps in conservation of animals and plants.

Worksheet

Life Skills

Go on a nature walk with your classmates and observe the diversity in plants and animals found in your area. Write a letter to the editor of your local newspaper discussing your observations and the steps that can be taken to conserve the biodiversity.

The Editor

____

____

____

Date: ________________

Subject: ____

____

____

____

____

____

____

____

____

____

____

____

____

____

____

Your sincerely,

____

____

Classification of Animals

3

What I shall learn

- General characteristics of animals
- Classification of animals into vertebrates and invertebrates
- Characteristic features of invertebrates
- Characteristic features of vertebrates
- Classification of animals based on their food
- Classification of animals based on their habitat

Kingdom Animalia
- Invertebrates (Absence of backbone)
- Vertebrates (Presence of backbone)

Remember

The branch of science concerned with the classification of living organisms is called **taxonomy**.

Introduction

In the five-kingdom classification system, animals have been classified under Kingdom Animalia. The general characteristics of the organisms under Kingdom Animalia are as follows.

- They are multicellular organisms. Their cells lack cell wall and have a well-defined nucleus.
- They are heterotrophs. That is, they cannot prepare their own food and depend on plants and other animals for food.
- They move from one place to another in search of food and shelter.

The animal kingdom is further divided into many groups and subgroups. Let us learn more about the classification of animals in this chapter.

Classification of Animals

The animal kingdom is broadly divided into two groups based on the presence or absence of a backbone: vertebrates and invertebrates. A vertebral column or spinal cord gives a definite shape to the body. **Vertebrates** are animals with a backbone and **invertebrates** are animals without a backbone. There are more invertebrates identified than vertebrates.

Invertebrates

Invertebrates do not have a vertebral column. They are generally soft-bodied, delicate creatures. Most of them are aquatic. Invertebrates have a variety of body shapes like round, flat, bag-shaped, thread-like, segmented, unsegmented and star-like. Invertebrates are divided into eight phyla (singular: phylum). Let us look at each phylum.

Do You Know?

The first animal to evolve was an invertebrate.

▲ Fig. 3.1 Barrel sponge

▲ Fig. 3.2 Tubular sponge

Phylum Porifera (Sponges)

- In Greek, *porus* means 'pores' and *ferre* means 'to bear'.
- These animals have a lot of pores on their body; hence, they are named as sponges.
- Sponges live as a single entity as well as in colonies.
- They are mostly found in marine habitats. Some sponges are found in freshwater habitats too.
- They are usually found attached to the bottom of the sea and cannot move from place to place.
- They do not have a mouth; they take in water containing food and oxygen through the tiny pores on their body.
- They have a large, central body cavity from where the water is released.
- Examples include Venus' flower basket, barrel sponge and tubular sponge (*Haliclona*).

Phylum Coelenterata (Cnidarians)

- In Greek, *knide* means 'nettle' or 'stinging cell'.
- The bodies of these organisms have radial symmetry (that is, their body can be divided into two equal halves through a central axis in more than one plane).
- They are mostly found in marine habitats attached to the bottom of the ocean as well as floating on water.
- The mouth is the only opening in the body. The mouth is surrounded by finger-like projections known as **tentacles**. The tentacles have stinging cells called **cnidoblasts**; hence, the name cnidarians.
- The tentacles help them to catch their prey and also to anchor themselves.
- Examples include *Hydra*, jellyfish, sea anemone and corals.

Challenge Yourself

Why should sponges be considered animals? How are sponges different from fungi?

▲ Fig. 3.3 Sea anemone

▲ Fig. 3.4 Jellyfish

Do You Know?

Jellyfish outdate dinosaurs and sharks in evolution, dating back to about 650 million years.

Phylum Platyhelminthes (Flatworms)

- In Greek, *platys* means 'flat' and *helminth* means 'worms'.
- The body of flatworms is flat, thin and long.

- They are unsegmented (that is, they have a smooth body surface) and bilaterally symmetrical (that is, their body can be divided into two identical halves through only one plane).
- A few of them are found in freshwater, while most of them are animal parasites (live inside hosts).
- Their mouth is the only opening on the body through which they take in food and excrete wastes. Hook-like structures called **suckers** surround their mouth.
- Examples include *Planaria*, tapeworm and blood fluke.

Do You Know?

Tapeworm is the most commonly found flatworm. It is a parasite that lives inside a host organism and derives food from it. It is usually found in the gut of human beings and cattle.

Phylum Nemathelminthes or Nematoda (Roundworms)

- In Greek, *nema* means 'thread' and *helminth* means 'worm'.
- Roundworms are both free-living as well as parasitic.
- They are found commonly in animal intestines.
- The body of roundworms is long, unsegmented, cylindrical and bilaterally symmetrical.
- They have two openings in the body, a mouth and an anus.
- Examples include *Ascaris* (roundworm), threadworm and hookworm.

▲ Fig. 3.5 *Planaria*

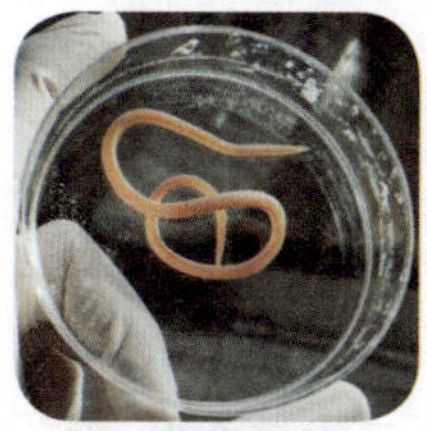

▲ Fig. 3.6 *Ascaris*

Phylum Annelida (Segmented Worms)

- In Greek, *annulus* means 'little ring' and *eidos* means 'form'.
- These organisms are found in moist soil and water.
- They have ring-like segments on the body surface.
- They have a body cavity and a digestive system with two openings – mouth and anus.
- They have special excretory organs known as **nephridia**.
- Examples include earthworm, leech, tubeworm and ragworm. Earthworms feed on dead and decaying substances in the soil. A leech is known as an **external parasite** as it sucks the blood of animals.

▲ Fig. 3.7 Leech

Revision Zone

Write T for True and F for False.

1. Organisms of Phylum Coelenterata have radial symmetry.
2. Hook-like structures called suckers are characteristic features of Phylum Porifera.
3. Leech is an example of an internal parasite.
4. Hookworms belong to Phylum Platyhelminthes.
5. Nemathelminthes are commonly known as roundworms.

Phylum Arthropoda (Animals That Have Jointed Legs)

- In Greek, *arthron* means 'a joint' and *podus* means 'foot'.
- It is one of the largest phyla. Arthropods are found in all habitats.
- They have a segmented body and jointed legs.
- The body is bilaterally symmetrical and has three main parts: head, thorax and abdomen.
- They have a protective hard shell covering their body called **exoskeleton**.
- They are further divided into four classes: crustaceans, insects, arachnids and myriapoda.

▲ Fig. 3.8 Lobster

▲ Fig. 3.9 Woodlouse

Crustaceans

- In Greek, *crusta* means 'hard shell' and *acea* means 'belonging to'.
- They are mostly found in marine habitats.
- They have a fused head and thorax, and two pairs of antennae on the head.
- They have an exoskeleton and many pairs of legs.
- Examples include lobster, crab, shrimp and woodlouse.

▲ Fig. 3.10 Grasshopper

▲ Fig. 3.11 Wasp

Insects

- They are found in soil, water and air.
- Their body is differentiated into head, thorax and an abdomen.
- All the body parts are covered by a single exoskeleton.
- They have three pairs of legs, a pair of antennae or feelers and usually two pairs of wings. There are some insects which have one pair of wings, and some insects like ant are wingless.
- Examples include grasshopper, wasp, cockroach, bee, mosquito and butterfly.

▲ Fig. 3.12 Spider

▲ Fig. 3.13 Scorpion

Arachnids

- In Greek, *arachne* means 'spider'.
- They are found on land.
- Their head and thorax is fused.
- They do not have wings or antennae.
- They have a jaw-like structure called **pincer**, an exoskeleton and four pairs of legs.
- Examples include tick, mite, spider and scorpion.

Myriapoda

- In Greek, *myriad* means 'ten thousand' and *podus* means 'feet'.
- They are found on land.
- Their body is divided into several segments, with one or two pairs of legs per segment.
- Examples include millipede (two pairs of legs per segment) and centipede (one pair of legs per segment).

Watch Out!

A centipede's bite is poisonous.

▲ Fig. 3.14 Centipede

▲ Fig. 3.15 Millipede

Phylum Mollusca (Animals That Have Shells and Soft Bodies)

- In Greek, *molluscus* means 'thin-shelled'.
- These soft-bodied animals are found in marine habitats, on seashores and on land.
- Their body is unsegmented and bilaterally symmetrical.
- Snails and oysters have a hard exoskeleton called **shell** to protect their soft bodies. Octopuses and slugs have a reduced internal shell.
- Examples include octopus, oyster, snail and squid.

▲ Fig. 3.16 Oyster

▲ Fig. 3.17 Slug

Phylum Echinodermata (Animals With a Spiny Skin)

- In Greek, *derma* means 'skin'.
- They are found in marine habitats.
- Their body is covered with a hard skin containing spines, and they have an endoskeleton.
- They move with the help of tube feet with structures called **suckers** present at their end.
- The adults are radially symmetrical, while larvae are bilaterally symmetrical.
- Examples include sea urchin, starfish, sea cucumber and brittle star.

▲ Fig. 3.18 Starfish

▲ Fig. 3.19 Sea cucumber

Revision Zone

Choose the correct answer for each of the following.

1. Identify the characteristic feature of arthropods.
   a. Endoskeleton b. Jointed legs c. Shells d. Suckers
2. Which of the following has tube feet?
   a. Starfish b. Octopus c. Millipede d. Centipede
3. Which of these molluscs has an internal shell?
   a. Sea urchin b. Sea cucumber c. Slugs d. Brittle star
4. Insects belong to Phylum
   a. Annelida b. Echinodermata c. Arthropoda d. Mollusca

Classification of Vertebrates

Vertebrates are animals with a backbone or a vertebral column that is made up of small bones called **vertebrae**. The vertebral column gives a definite shape and structure to organisms. In most animals, the vertebral column extends to form a tail. They have well-developed sense organs, and nervous and digestive systems. They have muscles and skeleton, and are capable of complex movements.

Vertebrates are further divided into five classes. Let us look at each class in detail.

▲ Fig. 3.20 Seahorse

▲ Fig. 3.21 Rohu

▲ Fig. 3.22 Salamander

▲ Fig. 3.23 Newt

▲ Fig. 3.24 Turtle

▲ Fig. 3.25 Crocodile

Pisces (Animals That Live in Water)

- In Greek, *pisces* means 'fish'.
- They are found in aquatic habitats.
- They have special organs called gills to breathe, which help them to take in the dissolved oxygen in water.
- They have a streamlined body and fins to help them swim.
- They are **cold-blooded**, that is, their body temperature varies according to the temperature of the surroundings.
- Eggs of pisceans are laid in water.
- Examples are rohu, eel, seahorse and shark.

Amphibia (Animals That Live on Land and in Water)

- In Greek, *amphi* means 'both' and *bios* means 'life'. They are found in both aquatic and terrestrial habitats.
- They breathe through their moist skin when present in water and through their lungs when present on land. Respiration through the skin is called **cutaneous respiration**.
- They are **cold-blooded** animals with smooth slippery skin.
- They reproduce by laying eggs in water.
- Examples are frog, newt and salamander.

Reptilia (Animals That Crawl)

- In Greek, *reptilis* means 'to creep'.
- Reptiles are found both on land and in water, but they are better suited to land than amphibians.
- They are **cold-blooded** animals. They breathe through their lungs.
- Their skin is covered with **scales** or **scutes** (such as the shell of a tortoise and the bony shield of a crocodile).
- They lay eggs on land and their young ones directly hatch into young adults without undergoing the larval stage.
- Examples are crocodile, lizard and turtle.

Aves (Animals With Feathers)

- In Greek, *aves* means 'birds'.
- They share a varied habitat such as land, water and trees.
- They breathe through lungs.

- They are **warm-blooded** animals, that is, their body temperature does not change with a change in the temperature of their surroundings.
- Most of them have forelimbs modified into a pair of wings to fly.
- They have a streamlined body covered with feathers and hollow bones that help them to fly.
- They have two legs (hind limbs) to walk, perch and catch their prey. They reproduce by laying eggs.
- Since they have beaks, they have no teeth.
- Examples include parrot, owl, crow and ostrich.

Some birds cannot fly. These are known as **flightless birds**. The smallest flightless bird is the island rail and the largest is the ostrich. Penguin, emu, cassowary, kiwi and rhea are other examples of flightless birds.

Do You Know?

Salamanders can regenerate a lost limb or tail.

▲ Fig. 3.26 Owl

▲ Fig. 3.27 Crow

Mammalia (Animals That Suckle Their Young Ones)

- In Greek, *mammalis* means 'of the breast'.
- Mammals are highly-evolved animals amongst vertebrates.
- In mammals, females have mammary glands that produce milk. They suckle their babies after giving birth.
- They are found on land and in water.
- They are **warm-blooded** animals with hair on their skin. They breathe through lungs.
- They have a well-developed brain. They also have external ears, nose, eyes and a set of teeth.
- They usually have two pairs of limbs. Some use all the four limbs as legs while others use one pair as legs and the other pair as hands.
- Examples include human being, cat, dog, cow and horse.

▲ Fig. 3.28 Cow and calf

▲ Fig. 3.29 Horse and pony

Revision Zone

Choose the correct answer for each of the following.

1. Which group of animals lives both on land and in water?
   a. Aves   b. Amphibia   c. Reptilia   d. Mammalia
2. The animals belonging to this phylum have hair on their body.
   a. Reptilia   b. Mammalia   c. Aves   d. Amphibia
3. Cutaneous respiration is breathing through
   a. gills   b. lungs   c. skin   d. mouth
4. The crocodile belong to the class
   a. Mammalia   b. Aves   c. Reptilia   d. Amphibia

Do You Know?

The duck-billed platypus is a mammal that lays eggs. It lives in a semi-aquatic habitat.

Bats are the only mammals that can fly. They have webbed wings that are an extension of their digits or fingers.

Classification Based on the Type of Nutrition

Nutrition is consuming (taking in) essential nutrients like carbohydrates, proteins, fats, vitamins and minerals. All animals need these nutrients for survival. The mode of consuming these nutrients varies from organism to organism. Animals are broadly divided into two groups based on the type of nutrition:

1. **Holozoic animals** consume plants or other animals as food. These animals are divided into three subgroups: herbivorous, carnivorous and omnivorous animals.
   - **Herbivorous animals** eat only plant and plant products. Examples include cow, sheep, goat, giraffe, elephant, deer and bison.
   - **Carnivorous animals** eat flesh of other animals. Examples include lion, tiger, cheetah, leopard, wolf and frog.
   - **Omnivorous animals** eat both animals and plants. Examples include chimpanzee, bear, crow and human being.
2. **Parasitic animals** like roundworms, tapeworms and head louse live inside the body or on the body surface of host animals and derive nutrition from them.

Classification Based on Habitat

Living things are adapted to their natural habitat. Animals can be classified into three groups based on the type of habitat: terrestrial, aquatic and arboreal.

Terrestrial Animals Animals that live entirely or predominantly on land are known as terrestrial animals. Ant, snail, tiger, elephant, cow and dog are some examples of terrestrial animals.

Aquatic Animals Animals that live entirely or predominantly in water are known as aquatic animals. Fish, octopus, dolphin, whale and squid are some examples of aquatic animals.

Arboreal Animals Animals that live on trees most of the time are known as arboreal animals. Monkey, squirrel, koala bear, panda and lemur are arboreal animals.

Keywords

Invertebrates: animals that do not have a vertebral column or spinal cord

Vertebrates: animals that have a vertebral column or spinal cord

Tentacles: the finger-like projections that surround the mouths of coelenterates

Nephridia: the excretory organs in organisms of Phylum Annelida

Exoskeleton: a hard outer covering on the body of certain organisms

Pincer: a jaw-like structure in Arachnids

Shell: a hard exoskeleton found in animals belonging to Phylum Mollusca

Suckers: the tube-like feet found in Phylum Echinodermata

Amphibians: animals that can live both on land and in water

Mammals: animals that suckle their young ones

In a Nutshell

- On the basis of presence or absence of backbone, animals can be divided into invertebrates and vertebrates.
- Invertebrates are classified into the following phyla: Porifera, Coelenterata, Platyhelminthes, Nemathelminthes, Annelida, Arthropoda, Mollusca and Echinodermata.
- Phylum Porifera has simple, multicellular organisms with pores all over their body.
- Phylum Coelenterata has animals with tentacles that have stinging cells called cnidoblasts.
- Phylum Platyhelminthes has flat, unsegmented worms and Phylum Nemathelminthes has round, unsegmented worms.
- Phylum Annelida has cylindrical, segmented worms with special excretory organs called nephridia.
- Phylum Arthropoda has animals with three pairs of jointed legs, and body divided into head, thorax and abdomen.
- Phylum Mollusca has animals with soft, unsegmented bodies and a hard shell. Phylum Echinodermata has marine animals with radially symmetrical body and sharp spines.
- Vertebrates are categorized into five classes: Pisces, Amphibia, Reptilia, Aves and Mammalia.
- Pisces are cold-blooded aquatic animals with streamlined bodies. They breathe through gills. Amphibians are cold-blooded animals that can live on land and in water.
- Reptiles are cold-blooded animals that breathe through lungs and lay eggs. Aves are warm-blooded animals that have feathers and most of them can fly. They lay eggs.
- Mammals are warm-blooded animals that give birth to babies and suckle them with milk.

Mind Map

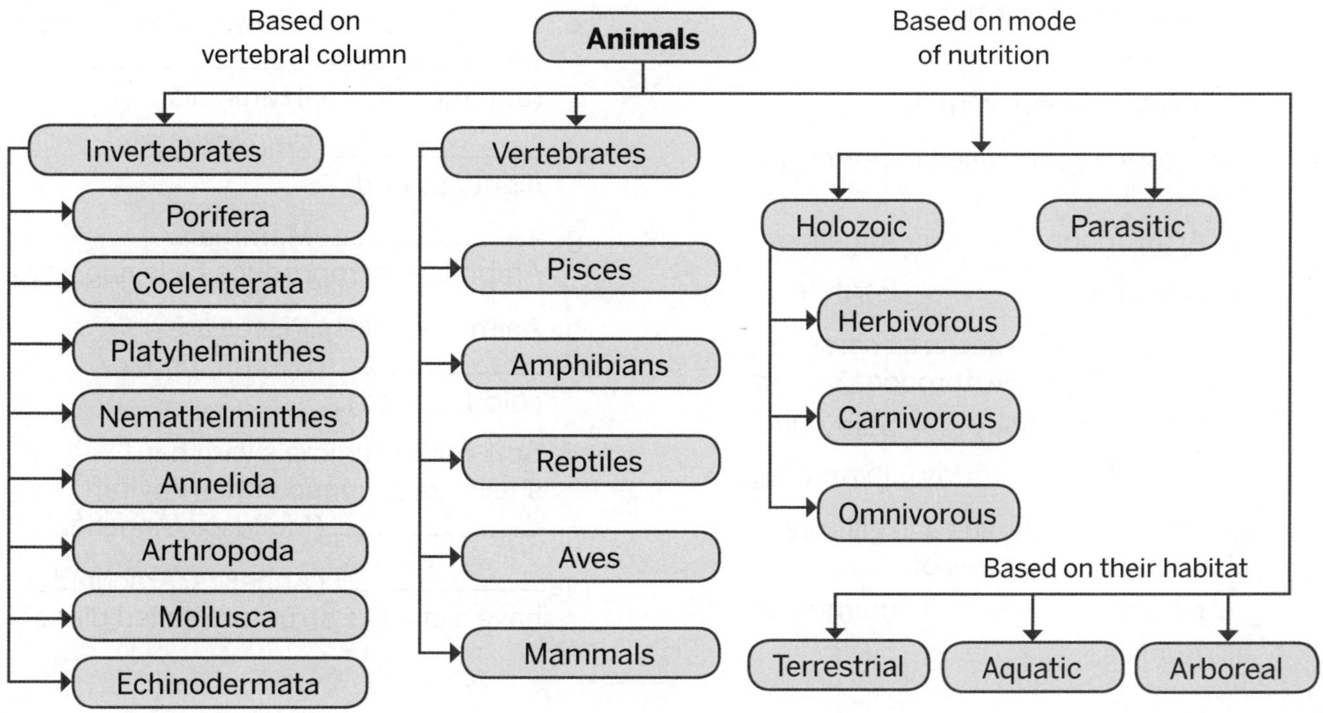

Exercise

1 Choose the correct answer for each of the following.

a. Which of these belongs to Phylum Porifera?
   i. *Haliclona* ii. Jellyfish
   iii. Roundworm iv. *Hydra*

b. Blood fluke belongs to
   i. Porifera ii. Platyhelminthes
   iii. Coelenterata iv. Nemathelminthes

c. Finger-like projections around the mouth of cnidarians are called
   i. flagella ii. tentacles
   iii. cilia iv. none of these

d. Which of the following is a characteristic feature of reptiles?
   i. Webbed feet ii. Scaled skin
   iii. Feather iv. Tentacles

e. Animals of Phylum Echinodermata are also known as
   i. soft-bodied animals
   ii. segmented worms
   iii. roundworms
   iv. spiny-skinned animals

f. Excretory organs called nephridia are present in
   i. Arthropoda ii. Annelida
   iii. Cnidarians iv. Porifera

g. Which of the following is a characteristic feature of Phylum Arthropoda?
   i. Segmented body ii. Spiny skin
   iii. Hard shell iv. Jointed legs

h. Streamlined body, fins and gills are characteristic features of
   i. pisces ii. mammals
   iii. reptiles iv. birds

i. Which of these is a cold-blooded animal that has slippery skin and can live on land and in water?
   i. Seahorse ii. Newt
   iii. Rohu iv. Eel

j. Animals that have hollow bones and streamlined bodies covered with feathers belong to
   i. Mammalia ii. Reptilia
   iii. Aves iv. Amphibia

2 Fill in the blanks.

a. Vertebrates that belong to the group ____________ (Pisces/Aves) can fly.

b. Cutaneous respiration in frogs takes place through ____________ (skin/gills).

c. ____________ (Holozoic/Parasitic) animals consume other animals.

d. ____________ (Carnivorous/ Omnivorous) animals consume both animals and plants.

e. Animals that live in trees most of the time are known as ____________ (aquatic/arboreal) animals.

f. ____________ (Emu/Owl) is a flightless bird.

g. ____________ (Mammals/ Amphibians) reproduce by laying eggs.

h. Animals of class Pisces are ____________ (warm-blooded/ cold-blooded).

i. Soft-bodied animals with hard shells are grouped under Phylum ____________ (Mollusca/Annelida).

j. ____________ (Annelids/Arachnids) have a jaw-like structure called pincer.

3. **Write T for True and F for False.**
   a. Frogs are cold-blooded animals.
   b. Human beings are mammals.
   c. Crocodiles lay eggs in water.
   d. Tentacles are present in flatworms.
   e. The turtle is a reptile.
   f. Annelids have a soft outer covering called endoskeleton.
   g. Animals of Phylum Porifera have radially symmetrical bodies.
   h. Mammals are cold-blooded animals with no hair on their skin.

4. **Differentiate between the following.**
   a. Porifera and Cnidarian
   b. Platyhelminthes and Nemathelminthes
   c. Amphibians and Pisces
   d. Arachnids and insects
   e. Molluscs and Echinoderms

5. **Choose the odd one out. Give reasons for your choice.**
   a. *Planaria*, tapeworm, earthworm, blood fluke
   b. *Haliclona*, *Hydra*, jellyfish, sea anemone
   c. Grasshopper, wasp, spider, mosquito
   d. Snail, octopus, oyster, starfish

6. **Answer the following questions in brief.**
   a. Give any two examples of crustaceans.
   b. Differentiate between a centipede and a millipede based on their number of legs per segment.
   c. Name the three body parts of an insect.
   d. What do you mean by an exoskeleton?
   e. Give any two examples of animal parasites.
   f. Explain the features of Echinodermata in brief.
   g. Animals belonging to Phylum Coelenterata are also known as cnidarians. Give reasons.
   h. What are pincers?
   i. What are tentacles?
   j. Give two examples of Myriapods.

7. **Answer the following questions in detail.**
   a. Explain the classification of animals based on their mode of nutrition.
   b. Write a note on Phylum Annelida.
   c. Write the characteristics of Phylum Coelenterata.
   d. Explain the characteristics of the Phylum Porifera.
   e. List the eight phyla of invertebrates. Give one example of each.
   f. Explain the characteristic features of Aves.
   g. Name different classes of Phylum Arthropoda. Give one characteristic feature and one example of each.
   h. Write short notes on amphibians and reptiles.

8. **Think and answer.**

   What are the different ways in which mammals maintain their body temperature?
   (Hint: Mammals are warm-blooded)

9. **Project**

   Prepare a list of common animals you know. Group them into terrestrial, aquatic and arboreal on a chart paper.

10. **In the Library**

    Find out why leeches are known as external parasites.

11. **In the Laboratory**

    Observe the specimens of animals that are preserved in the laboratory. Draw any four of them in your practical notebook.

12. **Thinking Beyond**

    Marsupials are mammals that are born incomplete. The young ones are carried by their mothers and nurtured until completely developed. Find out more about marsupials.

Worksheet

Subject Integration

Draw the diagram of one organism belonging to each of the phyla listed below. Also mention two characteristics of that phylum.

Plylum Porifera

Name of the organism: ____________________

Characteristics of phylum

1. ____________________
2. ____________________

Phylum Annelidaa

Name of the organism: ____________________

Characteristics of phylum

1. ____________________
2. ____________________

Phylum Arthropoda

Name of the organism: ____________________

Characteristics of phylum

1. ____________________
2. ____________________

Phylum Mollusca

Name of the organism: ____________________

Characteristics of phylum

1. ____________________
2. ____________________

Photosynthesis and Respiration in Plants

4

What I shall learn

- Autotrophic nutrition
  - Photosynthesis
  - Factors that affect photosynthesis
- Types of respiration
  - Aerobic respiration
  - Anaerobic respiration
- Respiration in plants
- Difference between photosynthesis and respiration

Introduction

To keep themselves alive, all living organisms perform basic functions known as life processes. These life processes include respiration, nutrition, excretion, response to stimuli, growth and repair and reproduction.

In this chapter, let us learn about the processes of photosynthesis and respiration in plants.

Autotrophic Nutrition

Organisms capable of preparing their own food are known as autotrophs. This type of nutrition is called **autotrophic nutrition**.

We know that green plants prepare their own food through the process of **photosynthesis**. Therefore, they are also called **producers** or **autotrophs**. Photosynthesis takes place in all the green parts of a plant. The cells in the green parts of the plant contain an organelle called **chloroplast**, which contains a green pigment called **chlorophyll**. This pigment helps in trapping sunlight, the main source of energy. Water is drawn from the roots to the leaf blades. The underside of leaves have tiny pores called **stomata** through which carbon dioxide is drawn from the air.

Some plants lack chlorophyll or grow in areas where they do not get enough sunlight. Such plants depend on other organisms for their food. This type of nutrition in which nutrients are obtained from other organisms is called **heterotrophic nutrition**. Organisms that follow the heterotrophic mode of nutrition are called **heterotrophs**.

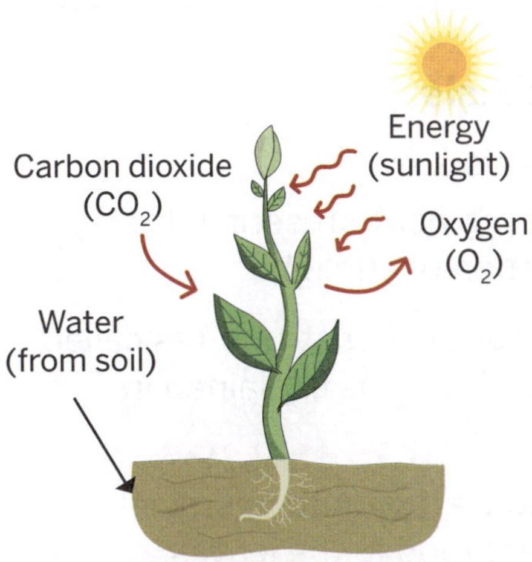

▲ Fig. 4.1 Green plants prepare their own food

Photosynthesis

Green plants use sunlight, chlorophyll, water and carbon dioxide to photosynthesize ('photo' means 'light' and 'synthesize' means 'to make').

$$\text{Carbon dioxide} + \text{Water} \xrightarrow[\text{Chlorophyll}]{\text{Sunlight}} \text{Glucose} + \text{Oxygen} + \text{Water}$$

$$6CO_2 + 12H_2O \xrightarrow[\text{Chlorophyll}]{\text{Sunlight}} C_6H_{12}O_6 + 6O_2 + 6H_2O$$

Six molecules of carbon dioxide and six molecules of water react in the presence of chlorophyll and sunlight to give one molecule of glucose and six molecules of oxygen. Oxygen and glucose thus formed are the products of photosynthesis. Oxygen is released through the stomata, and glucose is stored as starch and used by the plant for various metabolic activities.

Activity 1

Aim: To test for the presence of starch in a leaf after photosynthesis

Note: *This activity is to be performed as a teacher demonstration.*

Materials required: Iodine, dropper, Bunsen burner, test tube, beaker, alcohol, white tray and potted plant

Procedure:

1. Keep a healthy potted plant in darkness for about 24–48 hours.
2. Pluck a leaf out of this plant before you keep it out in sunlight. This is leaf A (the control).
3. Now, pluck another leaf from the plant after it has been in sunlight for at least one to two hours. This is leaf B (the experimental leaf).
4. Pour alcohol in a test tube and immerse the two leaves in it. Keep the test tube inside a 1 litre beaker containing water and heat it.

   (Caution: Alcohol is highly inflammable. It should never be heated directly.)

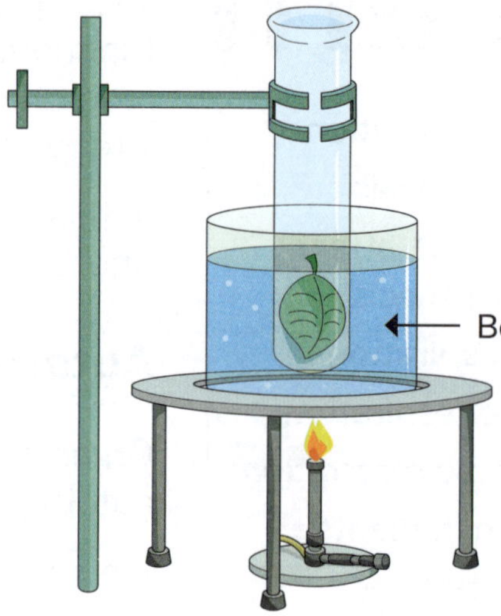

5. When the alcohol starts to boil, green colour comes off the leaves and the chlorophyll starts to dissolve in the alcohol.
6. Take out the leaves and wash them in water to remove the alcohol.
7. Place the leaves on the white tray and add a drop of iodine on the leaves using the dropper.

Observation: Leaf A does not change its colour, whereas in Leaf B the colour changes to blue–black, thereby indicating the presence of starch in it.

Challenge Yourself

1. What do you conclude from the above activity?
2. Why did Leaf A not change its colour whereas Leaf B did?
3. Why was the potted plant kept in dark for 24–48 hours?

Factors That Affect Photosynthesis

The factors that affect photosynthesis are:

Light: The chlorophyll or the green pigment present in the leaves of plants helps in the absorption of sunlight.

Leaf cells have special chlorophyll-containing structures called **chloroplasts**. The structure of chloroplasts is explained in Figure 4.2.

Chlorophyll absorbs sunlight and converts it into chemical energy, which is then used to prepare food in the leaves.

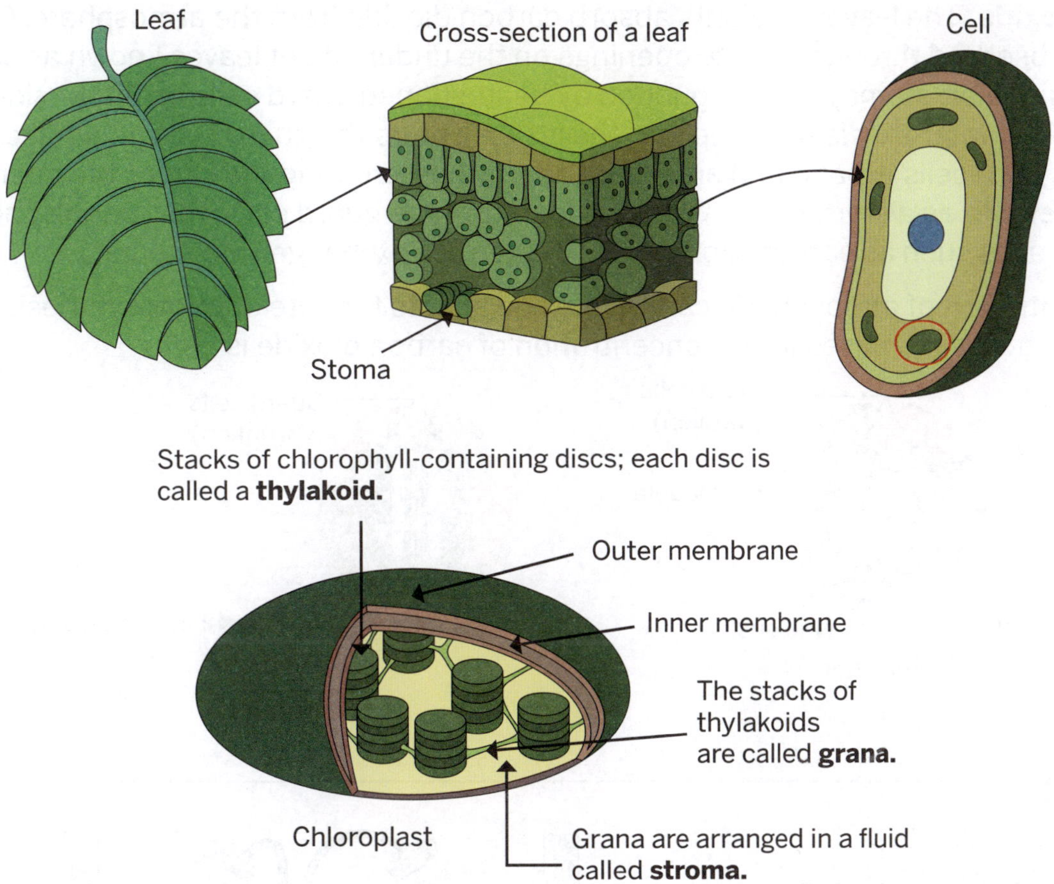

▲ Fig. 4.2 Chloroplasts in a plant cell

The intensity and duration of light affect the rate of photosynthesis. The rate of photosynthesis increases if the intensity of light increases.

Activity 2

Aim: To prove that light is required for the process of photosynthesis

Materials required: A potted plant, black paper and materials for the starch test

Procedure:

1. Keep a potted plant in a dark room for 24–48 hours.
2. Before keeping it out in sunlight, cover one of the leaves with black paper.
3. Leave the experimental set-up in the sunlight for 6–8 hours.
4. Pluck two leaves, the one that was covered with black paper and any other healthy leaf from the plant.
5. Now, test the leaves for starch as described in Activity 1.

Observation: The leaf covered with black paper shows a negative result for the starch test, whereas the other healthy leaf tests positive for starch.

Conclusion: The above experiment shows that sunlight is required for the process of photosynthesis.

Carbon dioxide: The leaves of plants absorb carbon dioxide from the atmosphere. Carbon dioxide is absorbed through minute openings on the underside of leaves known as **stomata**. Stomata (singular: stoma) are surrounded by bean-shaped guard cells on either side (Fig. 4.3). The water that is taken up into the leaves enters the guard cells and makes them swell. The guard cells expand and are pulled apart, thus, creating the gap or the opening, which we refer to as a stoma. When water is lost from the guard cells, they shrink and the gap is closed. Gases such as carbon dioxide and oxygen are exchanged via stomata.

The concentration of atmospheric carbon dioxide affects the rate of photosynthesis. The rate of photosynthesis increases if the concentration of carbon dioxide is high.

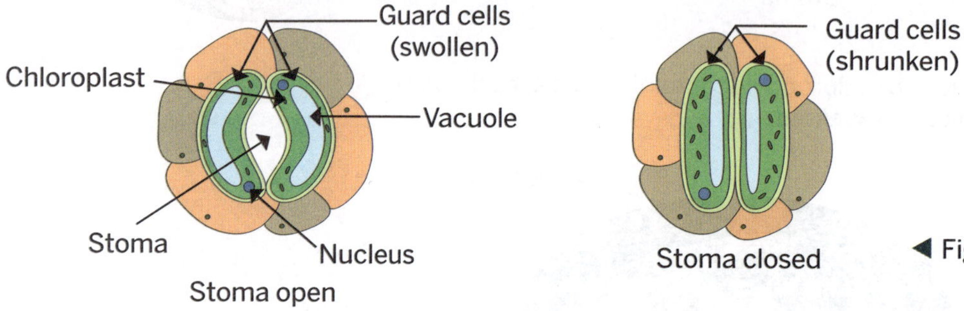

◀ Fig. 4.3 Structure of stomata

Activity 3

Aim: To demonstrate that carbon dioxide is required for photosynthesis

Materials required: Potted plant, two conical flasks, split corks, stands, water, potassium hydroxide and materials for starch test

Procedure:

Keep the potted plant in darkness/indoors for 24–48 hours.

Use this plant as given below.

1. Take two conical flasks. One conical flask marked A should contain potassium hydroxide and another marked B should contain water.
2. Insert one leaf of the potted plant into each flask through the split corks as shown in the picture. Arrange the set-up as shown in the figure. Take care not to immerse the leaves in the liquids.

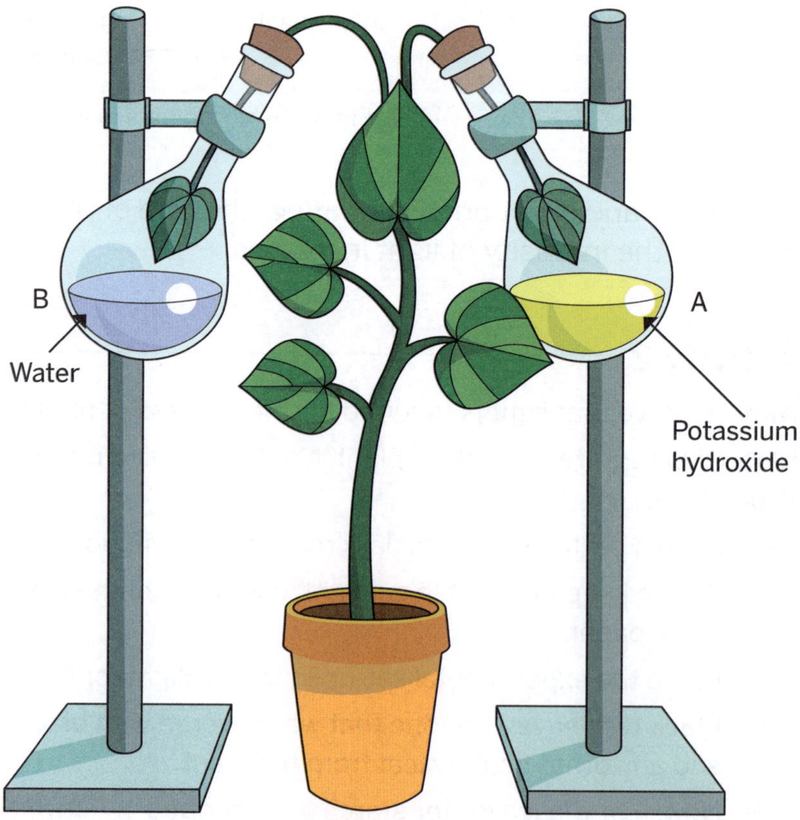

3. Leave the experimental set-up near a window or in sunlight for a few hours.
4. Pluck out both the leaves from the plant and test for starch as discussed in Activity 1.

Observation: The leaf from the set-up marked B turns blue–black due to the presence of starch, whereas the other one from flask A does not show any change in its colour.

Conclusion: Carbon dioxide necessary for photosynthesis is absorbed by the potassium hydroxide in flask A. Photosynthesis does not take place due to the absence of carbon dioxide. Starch is not formed. This is confirmed by the negative result of the starch test. Flask B contained water and thus, CO_2 was available. Starch was formed and it was confirmed by the positive result of the starch test.

Activity 4

Aim: To prove that chlorophyll is required for photosynthesis

Materials required: Iodine solution, potted plant with variegated leaves and materials for starch test

Procedure:

1. Keep the potted plant in darkness for 24 to 48 hours. Then expose it to sunlight for 4-6 hours.
2. Take a large, healthy leaf from the plant.
3. Draw the leaf in your notebook, carefully marking the areas on the leaf where chlorophyll is not present (or vice versa).
4. Perform the starch test as given in Activity 1.
5. Compare the colour of iodine seen on the leaf with your diagram. Where do you see the blue–black portions on the leaf?

▲ A plant with variegated leaves

Observation: Only those parts of a leaf, which are green in colour due to the presence of chlorophyll show the colour change for the starch test.

Conclusion: Chlorophyll is required for plants to make their food.

Temperature: The temperature between 20°C and 30°C is optimum for photosynthesis. If the temperature is higher than the optimum temperature range, it destroys the enzymes involved in the process.

Water and minerals: The root system in plants helps in the absorption of water and minerals from the soil. These are carried to the other parts of the plant through tubular structures called **xylem**.

Stomata open when water is available. Availability of water increases the rate of photosynthesis, whereas reduced water availability reduces the rate of photosynthesis as well as closes the stomata, thus, stopping the exchange of gases.

Respiration

All living beings need food as a source of energy to carry out various life processes. In the previous chapter, we learned how the process of digestion breaks down food into simple molecules like glucose. The process of **respiration** involves the oxidation of food (glucose) to produce water, carbon dioxide and energy.

Glucose + Oxygen ⟶ Water + Carbon dioxide + Energy

The energy released is stored and used by the body in the form of a chemical substance called **adenosine triphosphate** (ATP). ATP is also called the **energy currency** of a cell.

Types of Respiration

Intake of oxygen is one of the first steps of respiration. However, respiration can happen in the absence of oxygen also.

When food (glucose) is broken down in the presence of oxygen, it is called **aerobic respiration**.

$$\underset{\text{Glucose}}{C_6H_{12}O_6} + \underset{\text{Oxygen}}{6O_2} \longrightarrow \underset{\text{Carbon dioxide}}{6CO_2} + \underset{\text{Water}}{6H_2O} + \underset{\text{Energy}}{38\text{ ATP}}$$

Carbon dioxide is released and water is used up for other cellular functions. Aerobic respiration is the most common type of respiration exhibited by most organisms. It is also the most efficient form of respiration.

When food is broken down in the absence of oxygen, it is called **anaerobic respiration**. Anaerobic respiration is exhibited in some organisms such as yeast and certain bacteria.

$$\underset{\text{Glucose}}{C_6H_{12}O_6} \longrightarrow \underset{\text{Ethyl alcohol}}{2C_2H_5OH} + \underset{\text{Carbon dioxide}}{2CO_2} + \underset{\text{Energy}}{2\text{ ATP}}$$

Anaerobic respiration in yeast is responsible for the fluffiness of bread, idli and dosa batter. The naturally present yeast causes fermentation in the batter leading to the escape of carbon dioxide and leading to small holes in the bread, thus, creating fluffiness.

Anaerobic respiration takes place only for short durations. Aerobic respiration produces more energy than anaerobic respiration.

The muscle cells in our body normally carry out aerobic respiration. But when we run fast or exercise vigorously, the muscle cells work faster and require instant energy. To meet this energy demand, the muscle cells switch to anaerobic respiration. But in this case, instead of alcohol, lactic acid is produced. The partial breakdown of glucose produces lactic acid.

Glucose ⟶ Lactic acid + Energy

Table 4.1 Differences between aerobic and anaerobic respiration

Aerobic respiration	Anaerobic respiration
Oxidation of glucose in the presence oxygen	Oxidation of glucose in the absence of oxygen
Occurs in plants, animals, human beings and microorganisms	Occurs in organisms when there is a condition of insufficient oxygen, and in some microorganisms
Glucose is broken down completely	Glucose is broken down partially
More energy is released	Less energy is released

Activity 5

Aim: To prove that anaerobic respiration takes place in the absence of oxygen, while aerobic respiration takes place in the presence of oxygen

Materials required: Germinating seeds, lime water, two test tubes, two conical flasks, stoppers, bent glass tubes, short tubes, oil, warm water, yeast and glucose

Procedure: Distribute lime water equally into the test tubes (take the help of your teacher to make sure that it does not come in contact with the carbon dioxide in the air).

Experimental set-up 1: Place 30 g of germinating seeds in one of the conical flasks. Cover the conical flask with the two-holed stopper. Insert a bent glass tube into one hole and the short tube into the other hole. Connect the bent tube to a test tube having lime water through the one-holed stopper.

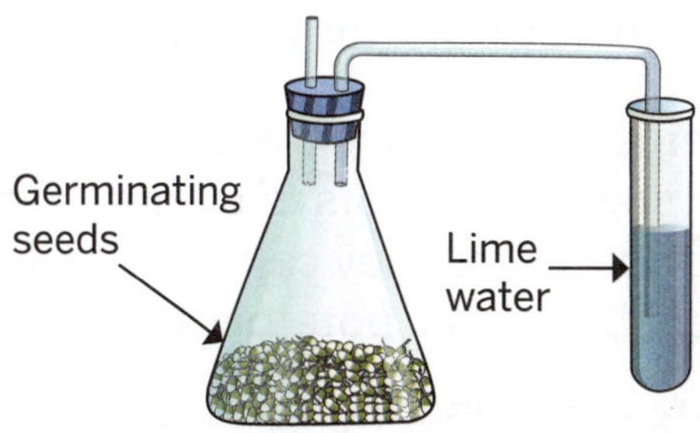

Experimental set-up 1

Experimental set-up 2: Pour the warm water into another conical flask and add glucose and yeast. Mix well. Pour oil over the surface of the solution (to prevent the entry of air). Do not shake the set-up once the oil is poured. Close it with the one-holed stopper by fitting it with a bent glass tube. Connect the bent tube to a test tube having lime water through a one-holed stopper.

Experimental set-up 2

Leave the two experimental set-ups undisturbed for 15–20 minutes. Make sure that the bent tube is immersed in the lime water in both the cases.

Observation: In both the experimental set-ups, lime water gradually turns milky.

Conclusion: In experimental set-up 1, the germinating seeds are kept in an aerobic condition. The lime water turning milky is an indication of the release of carbon dioxide. In the experimental set-up 2, the yeast cells are kept in an anaerobic condition, but still the lime water turns milky. This is because yeast cells are capable of respiring even in anaerobic conditions.

Revision Zone

Fill in the blanks.

1. Respiration happening in the presence of oxygen is called ____________.
2. Respiration happening in the absence of oxygen is called ____________.
3. During vigorous exercise, the muscle cells break down glucose into ____________.
4. The abbreviation ATP stands for ____________.
5. The process responsible for fluffiness of bread is ____________.

Respiration in Plants

Plants also respire by taking in oxygen and giving out carbon dioxide.

Stomata: The leaves of most plants have tiny pores called **stomata** mostly on the underside. Guard cells on either side of the stomata regulate their opening and closing.

Stomata are also involved in the processes of photosynthesis and transpiration. Stomata bring about the exchange of oxygen and carbon dioxide in plant cells.

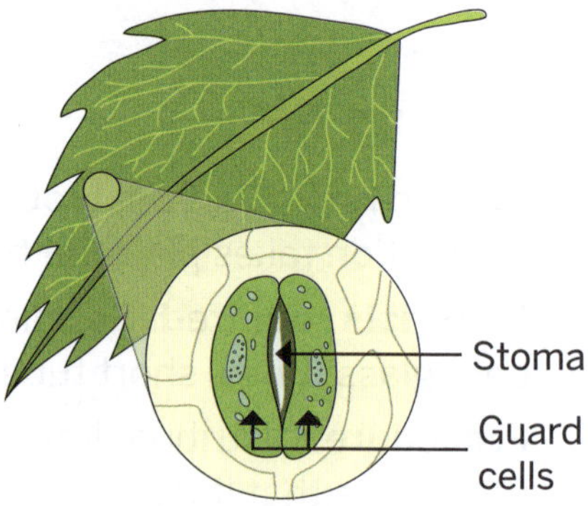

▲ Fig. 4.4 Stomata on the underside of a leaf

Lenticels: Lenticels are openings found on the barks of trees or stems and roots of plants. They help in the exchange of gases between the plant and the atmosphere. They can be raised, circular, oval or elongated. Even some fruits like apples and vegetables like potatoes have lenticels on them.

Pneumatophores or breathing roots are an adaptation of roots in trees usually found in mangroves in swampy areas. These trees are partially submerged, which makes gaseous exchange difficult. These roots come up from the submerged main roots in the water. They have lenticels on the surface for breathing.

Diffusion: Diffusion is a process of gaseous exchange through the surface of leaves and stems of herbaceous plants.

Difference Between Photosynthesis and Respiration

Photosynthesis utilizes carbon dioxide, water and sunlight in the presence of chlorophyll to produce food (glucose) and oxygen is released into the atmosphere. This takes place only during the day because the process needs sunlight.

Respiration in plants takes place all the time; hence, during the daytime plants use a part of the oxygen produced during photosynthesis for respiration. This oxygen is used to break down complex food materials and produce energy and carbon dioxide.

The amount of carbon dioxide produced due to respiration is not sufficient for photosynthesis and hence, carbon dioxide is absorbed from the atmosphere.

Table 4.2 Differences between respiration and photosynthesis

Respiration	Photosynthesis
It is one of the characteristic features of living things.	Green plants use this process to prepare their own food.
It takes place in the cells of plants, animals, human beings and microorganisms.	It takes place in the cells of plants that contain chlorophyll.
Oxygen is absorbed to break down the complex food that is consumed.	Oxygen is released during this process.
Carbon dioxide is exhaled during respiration.	Carbon dioxide is required for this process.
Energy is obtained through the break down of the consumed food.	Sunlight is the source of energy to produce food.

Keywords

Photosynthesis: the process of preparing food in plants using carbon dioxide, water and sunlight in the presence of chlorophyll

Chlorophyll: the green pigment that helps in the absorption of sunlight

Chloroplast: the organelles in plant cells that contain chlorophyll

Stomata: the openings found mostly on the underside of leaves, through which plants take in and give out carbon dioxide and oxygen

Thylakoid: chlorophyll-containing discs inside chloroplasts

Grana: stacks of thylakoids arranged inside chloroplasts

Respiration: the process of breaking down of food into carbon dioxide, water and energy in a living being

ATP: abbreviation for adenosine triphosphate

Aerobic respiration: a type of respiration taking place in the presence of oxygen

Anaerobic respiration: a type of respiration taking place in the absence of or in insufficient oxygen

Lenticels: Openings found on the barks of trees or stems and roots of plants that help in the exchange of gases between the plant and the atmosphere

In a Nutshell

- Green plants are autotrophs. They prepare their own food using sunlight, water and carbon dioxide in the presence of the green pigment chlorophyll.
- Six molecules of carbon dioxide and six molecules of water react in the presence of chlorophyll and sunlight to give one molecule of glucose and six molecules of oxygen.
- Oxygen and glucose thus formed are the products of photosynthesis. Oxygen is released through the stomata, and glucose is stored as starch and used by the plant for various metabolic activities.
- Respiration involves the oxidation of food (glucose) to produce water, carbon dioxide and energy.
- The energy released is stored and used by the body in the form of a chemical substance called adenosine triphosphate (ATP). ATP is also called the energy currency of a cell.
- The food prepared in the leaves is transported to other parts of the plants through phloem tissues.
- The rate of photosynthesis is affected by factors such as light, content of carbon dioxide in the atmosphere, temperature and the presence of water and minerals in the soil.
- Aerobic respiration takes place in the presence of oxygen and anaerobic respiration takes place in the absence of oxygen.
- Stomata in plants involved in the processes of photosynthesis and respiration. They bring about the exchange of oxygen and carbon dioxide in plant cells.

Mind Map

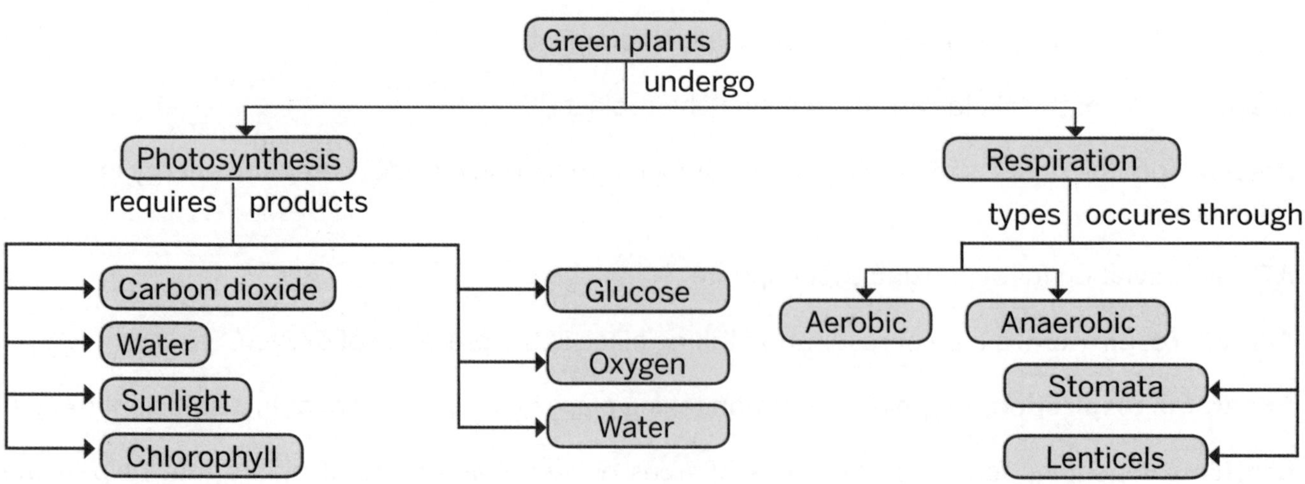

Exercise

1 Choose the correct answer for each of the following.

a. Stomata are present mostly on the
   i. underside of a leaf
   ii. upper side of a leaf
   iii. mid rib of a leaf
   iv. leaf margin

b. Which gas is released during photosynthesis?
   i. Nitrogen ii. Oxygen
   iii. Carbon dioxide iv. Hydrogen

c. Chlorophyll is a
   i. colourless substance
   ii. red pigment
   iii. green pigment
   iv. plant hormone

d. Which of these helps to trap sunlight?
   i. Oxygen ii. Chlorophyll
   iii. Carbon dioxide iv. Stomata

e. The chlorophyll containing structures in leaf cells are called
   i. tonoplasts ii. chloroplasts
   iii. leucoplasts iv. thermoplasts

f. The process of respiration involves
   i. oxidation of food
   ii. reduction of food
   iii. absorption of food
   iv. accumulation of food

g. How many molecules of ATP are generated at the end of an aerobic respiration involving 2 molecules of glucose?
   i. 38 ATP ii. 76 ATP
   iii. 19 ATP iv. 12 ATP

h. Respiration in plants occurs
   i. during day time
   ii. during night time
   iii. in vacuum
   iv. all the time

i. Which of the following fruits have lenticels?
   i. Banana ii. Mango
   iii. Apple iv.Strawberry

2 Fill in the blanks.

a. Iodine turns ______________ (blue–black/reddish brown) in the presence of starch.

b. Chlorophyll helps in the absorption of ______________ (water/light).

c. Stomata ______________ (open/close) when water is available.

d. The ideal temperature for photosynthesis is between ______________ (40–50°C/20–30°C).

e. Plants take in carbon dioxide and oxygen from ______________ (air/soil).

f. Oxidation of glucose requires ______________ (carbon dioxide/oxygen).

g. One of the products formed during the fermentation process is ______________ (alcohol/water).

h. ______________ (Stomata/Lenticels) are involved in both photosynthesis and respiration.

i. ______________ (Yeast/Muscle) cells carry out aerobic respiration.

3 Write T for True and F for False.

a. The rate of photosynthesis increases as the intensity of light decreases.

b. Plants prepare food only in the form of starch.

c. Energy produced during respiration is stored in the form of ATP.

d. Carbon dioxide is given out during respiration.

e. During photosynthesis, carbon dioxide is released.

f. Six molecules of carbon dioxide react with twelve molecules of water to give one molecule of glucose.

g. The green pigment chlorophyll is present inside mitochondria.

h. Plants that depend on other sources for food are called autotrophs.

i. Stoma has guard cells around it.

4 Define the following terms.

a. Photosynthesis

b. Respiration

c. Aerobic respiration

d. Anaerobic respiration

e. Energy currency

5 Differentiate between the following.

a. Aerobic and anaerobic respiration

b. Autotrophs and heterotrophs

c. Photosynthesis and respiration

6 Answer the following questions in brief.

a. What are the cell organelles involved in the process of photosynthesis?

b. List the factors that affect photosynthesis.

c. Write the importance of chlorophyll in the process of photosynthesis.

d. How is carbon dioxide taken in by plants?

e. What is the full form of ATP?

f. What is the main product of anaerobic respiration?

7 Answer the following questions in detail.

a. Explain the structure of a chloroplast with the help of a diagram.

b. Explain the structure and function of stomata with the help of a diagram.

c. List the materials required by a leaf to photosynthesize efficiently. How are these obtained by the plant?

d. Write the procedure to test a green leaf for the presence of starch.

e. Write a note on respiration in plants.

f. Describe an experiment to show that anaerobic respiration takes place in the absence of oxygen and aerobic respiration takes place in the presence of oxygen.

8 Think and answer.

a. What happens to the plant if a part of the bark is removed?

(Hint: Phloem tissues are present in the barks of trees.)

b. Can you guess what would happen if a potted plant having underground roots is overwatered?

(Hint: The root hairs have tiny pores open for respiration.)

9 Project

Germinate some seeds. Plant them in a tray with soil mixed with humus. Sprinkle water to add moisture to the plantlets regularly. Observe the tiny root hair that develop after a week.

Worksheet

1 Label the diagram of photosynthesis given below.

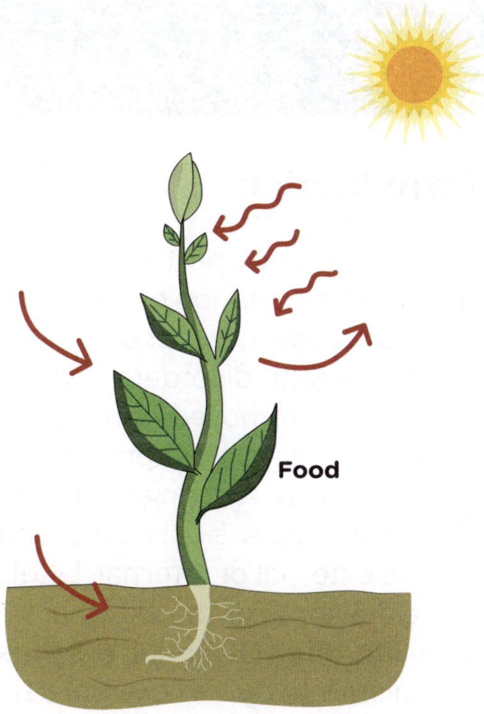

2 Life Skills

We should take care not to harm plants. If we pluck out the leaves of the plants, they lose their 'food factories'. At times, people who visit parks carve their names or doodle on the barks of the trees. Such destructive activities can disrupt the growth of the trees or cause fungal infections. Plants are important to us in many ways. The most important way in which plants help us is by producing oxygen during photosynthesis. We must, therefore, take care of plants. We must plant more and more trees and nurture them.

3 Given below is a list of plants. Find out the mode of nutrition for each and also what are they called. (One is done for you.)

Plant	Mode of nutrition	What are they called?
Cuscuta	It sucks food from other plants through special roots called haustoria.	Parasitic plant
Rafflesia		
Indian pipe		
Pitcher plant		

Excretory System and Nervous System

5

What I shall learn

- Excretion in human beings
  - Renal excretory system
  - Disorders of the urinary system
- Human nervous system
  - Role of nervous system in control and coordination
  - Structure and function of nerve cell
  - Structure and function of the brain and spinal cord

Introduction

The human body performs many functions like respiration, digestion, circulation etc. Some waste products are generated in these processes. Accumulation of wastes in the body leads to many health disorders. Therefore, these wastes need to be regularly removed from the body. The excretory system in humans plays an important role in removing these wastes from the body. A change in the environment to which an organism reacts is called a **stimulus** (plural: stimuli). Stimuli can be external or internal. Light, sound, smell, pain, touch and taste are some of the external stimuli we come across in our daily life. Internal stimuli are those that come from within the organism's body. For example, hunger, thirst and sleep.

The reaction of an organism to a stimulus is called a **response**. For example, if we accidentally touch a hot object, we respond by moving the hand away from that object.

Our responses to internal and external stimuli are controlled by the **nervous system**.

In this chapter, let us learn about the excretory system and the nervous system, and their functions.

Excretion in Human Beings

The amount of waste products produced in the human body is higher than in plants. Activities involving respiratory and digestive systems are the main contributors to the formation of waste products in the body. Table 5.1 gives the various ways in which these waste products are excreted.

Table 5.1 Waste products in humans

Waste product	Organ involved	Description
Carbon dioxide	Lungs	The gaseous exchange between blood and alveoli happens in the lungs. Carbon dioxide, the waste product of respiration, is exhaled through the nose.

Waste product	Organ involved	Description
Urine	Kidney	Urine is a human waste that is the product of the activities in the cells. These wastes are carried by blood and extracted by the kidney in the form of urine.
Sweat	Skin	Sweating is a process that helps the body to remove excess water and salts present in the body. During this process, it maintains the temperature of the body by reducing the body's temperature.

Renal Excretory System

The renal excretory system is one of the systems responsible for the removal of wastes from the human body.

During the various metabolic processes in the body, waste products like urea are produced that are carried in the blood. These waste products are filtered from the blood in kidneys; hence, kidneys play a major role in the renal excretory system.

The kidneys are aided by other organs like the ureter, urinary bladder and urethra.

Know the Scientist

Dr. Joseph E Murray was the first person to transplant a kidney from a healthy person to a patient suffering from kidney disorder. For his pioneering work, he was presented with the Nobel Prize in Physiology or Medicine in the year 1990.

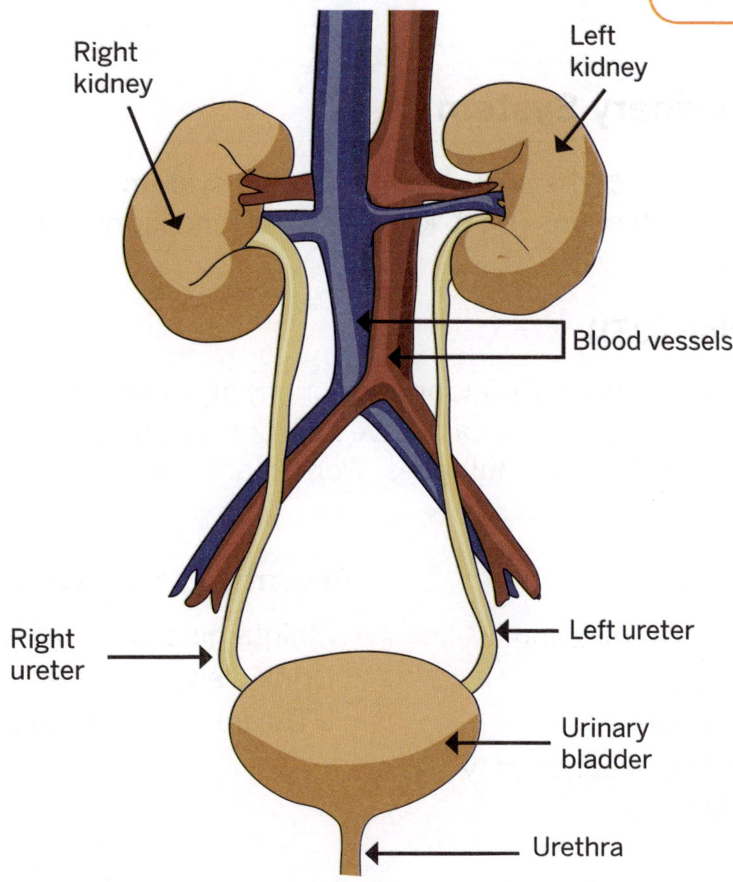

▲ Fig. 5.1 Renal excretory system

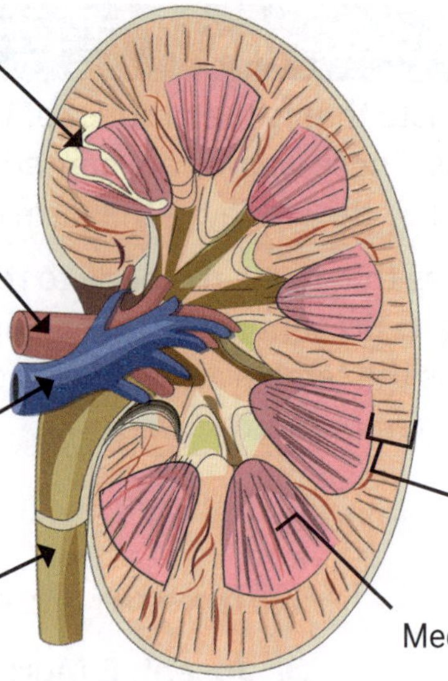

▲ Fig. 5.2 Structure of a kidney

Kidneys: Kidneys are brownish, bean-shaped organs, placed on either sides of the spinal cord or the backbone. A kidney is approximately 4 inches in length and 2 inches in width. Each kidney is connected with blood vessels that carry blood with the waste products in them. Another blood vessel is connected to take away the blood that is free of waste products.

The longitudinal section of a kidney shows a dark outer region called **cortex** and a light inner region called **medulla**.

Kidneys have a network of coiled tubes called **nephrons** that filter out wastes from the blood. Nephrons are called the structural and functional units of the kidneys.

Ureter: A ureter is connected to each kidney. The tubules of the nephrons carry the wastes to the ureter. From the ureter, the urine moves into the urinary bladder.

Urinary Bladder: It is a sac that stores the urine for a short period of time. It is connected to the two ureters.

Urethra: This is the passage that moves the urine out of the urinary bladder and out of the body.

Disorders of the Urinary System

Urinary system disorders affect the organs of the urinary system - kidneys, urinary bladder and ureters. Urinary tract infections (UTI), kidney stones and kidney failure are the commonly found urinary disorders.

Urinary tract infection (UTI)

These infections affect the upper part (kidney infection) or lower part of the urinary tract (bladder infection). The most common causative microorganism is *Escherichia coli*. It enters the bladder through the urethra and multiplies. Women are more prone to UTIs because of their anatomy.

Symptoms

- A burning sensation while urinating
- Frequent urge to urinate
- Pain in the lower abdomen
- Fever or chills (a sign the infection may have reached your kidneys)

Prevention and Treatment

- Maintaining personal hygiene
- Drink plenty of water
- UTIs are usually treated with antibiotics

Kidney Stones

Kidney stones are hard composition of minerals or salts found in urinary tract. Usually these stones are formed in the kidneys and then pass into the urinary tract through the stream of urine. A stone of size more than 5 millimeters can cause blockage in ureters. The major factors for stone formation are low fluid intake and high intake of animal protein, sugars and sodium.

Do You Know?

Cranberry juice prevents recurrence of UTI because it contains certain bio-compounds that prevent sticking of *E.coli* to the walls of the urinary bladder.

Symptoms

- Severe pain at the back and lower abdomen
- Pain during urination
- Urge to urinate frequently
- Nausea and vomiting

Prevention and Treatment

- Drinking plenty of water
- Avoiding high protein, sugar or salt diet
- Medication to relieve pain
- Medical procedures to remove stones

Nervous System

External activities such as movement and locomotion and internal activities such as metabolism in our body are mainly coordinated by the nervous system. **Brain**, **spinal cord** and a network of **nerves** are the organs of the nervous system, which help us in responding to stimuli.

Our **sense organs** like eye, ear, nose, skin and tongue help in detecting stimuli. Messages from our sense organs are taken to the brain by the nerves. This is similar to electrical signals being passed through electrical wires.

The messages passed through the nervous system are called **nerve impulses**. The brain also sends nerve impulses in return to the stimuli to muscles and glands of the body, which show the response.

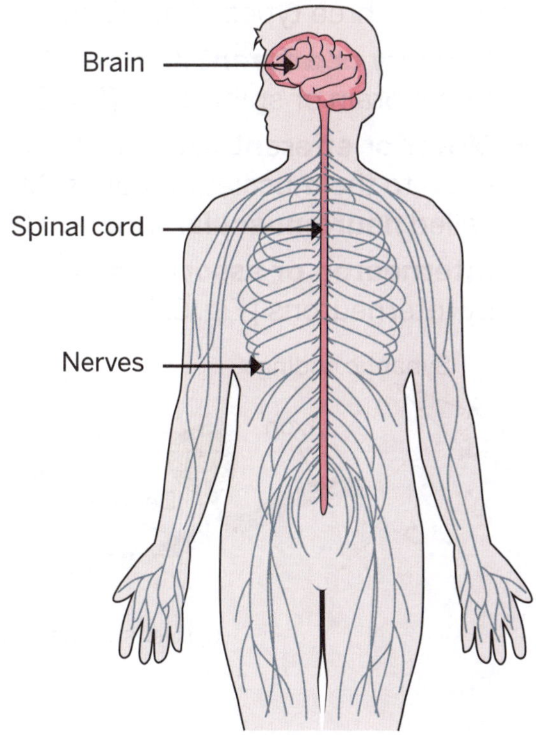

▲ Fig. 5.3 Nervous system

Nerves

Nerve cells are the basic unit of the nervous system. A nerve cell is also called **neuron**.

Structure of a Neuron

Figure 5.4 shows the structure of a neuron. A neuron contains a nucleus and the cell body extends to form branched structures called **dendrons**. Dendrons branch out further into structures called **dendrites**. One of the dendrites elongates from the cell body to form a tail-like structure called **axon**.

Wonder!

There are more nerve cells in the human body than the number of stars in the Milky Way galaxy.

Axon is insulated and protected by a sheath-like structure called **myelin sheath**. The myelin sheath is discontinuous at certain places. These places are called **nodes of Ranvier**. The junction between two neurons (the dendrite of one neuron and the axon terminal of another) is called a **synapse**.

Functions of dendrite, axon and myelin sheath are:

- The messages or nerve impulses are received by the dendrites.
- The axon transmits the nerve impulses to different neurons, muscles and glands.
- Myelin sheath insulates the axon and increases the rate of transmission of nerve signals or impulse.

Nerve impulses pass at a speed of 100 metres per second. A nerve can, however, conduct about 1000 nerve impulses each second.

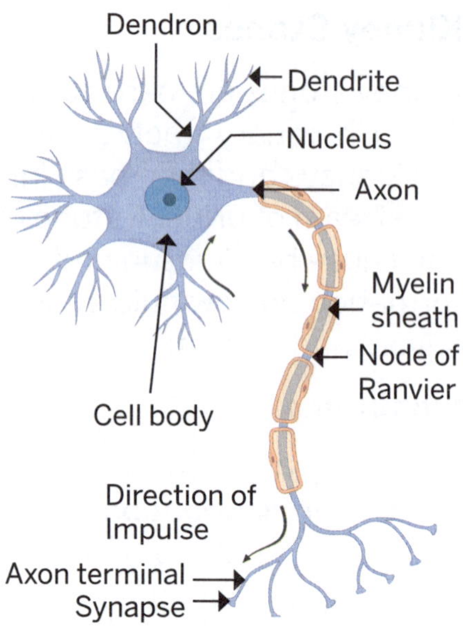

▲ Fig. 5.4 Neuron

Types of Neurons

There are three types of neurons:

- **Sensory or afferent neuron**: These neurons carry nerve impulses from the sense organs to the brain or spinal cord [Fig. 5.5 (a)].
- **Motor or efferent neuron**: These neurons carry nerve impulses from the spinal cord or brain to the muscles or glands. Motor neurons are connected to the muscles at junctions called **neuromuscular junction** [Fig. 5.5 (b)].
- **Interneuron or association neuron**: Afferent neuron and efferent neuron are connected by interneurons [Fig. 5.5 (c)].

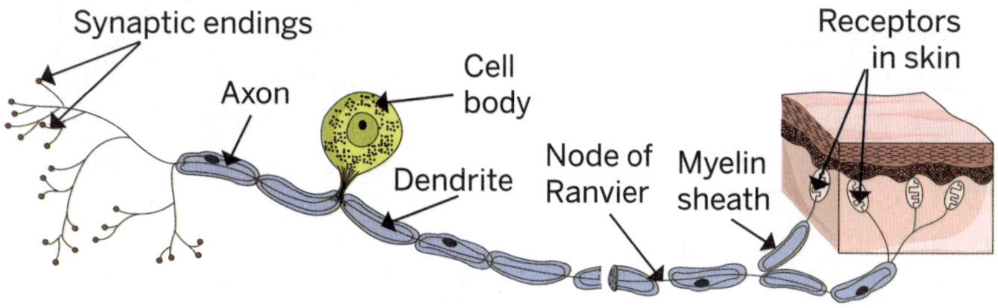

(a) Sensory neuron

Do You Know?

In a human embryo, about 2,50,000 nerve cells are made each minute.

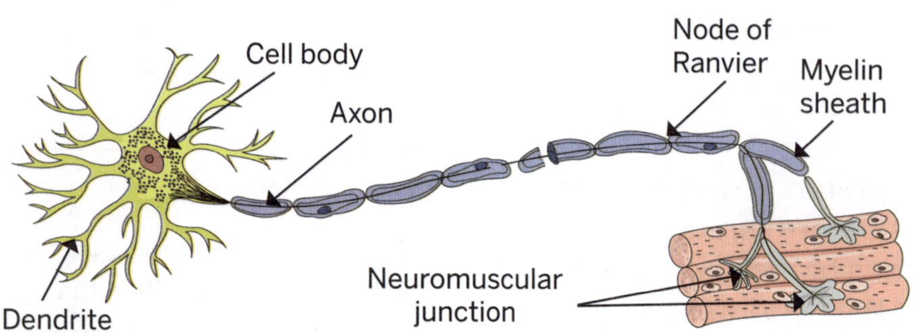

(b) Motor neuron

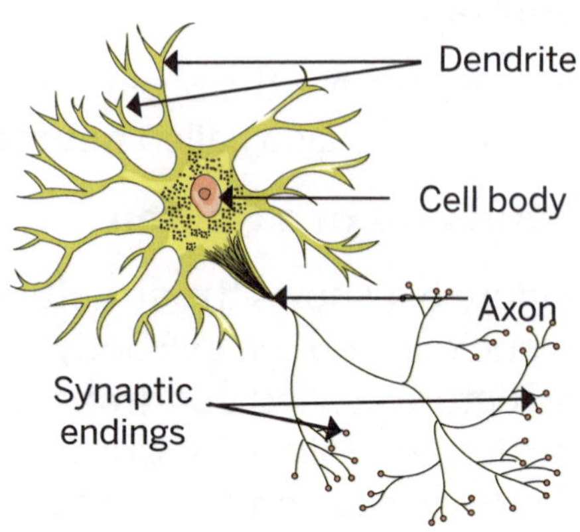

(c) Interneuron

▲ Fig. 5.5 Types of nerve cells

Human Nervous System

The human nervous system can be divided into central nervous system and peripheral nervous system.

Do You Know?

There are about 30,000 million neurons in our body.

Central Nervous System

Central nervous system is made up of the brain and the spinal cord.

Brain: The **brain** is located in the head inside the skull. The brain is protected by the bones of the skull and by a covering of three thin membranes called **meninges**. A fluid called **cerebrospinal fluid** present between the meninges protects the brain from shocks and injury.

The brain has three main parts:

- **Cerebrum**: The largest part of the brain is known as cerebrum. The surface of cerebrum has many foldings called **furrows** and **ridges**, which increase the surface area of the brain to contain more nerve cells.

The cerebrum is divided into left and right **cerebral hemispheres** with a deep furrow between them [Fig. 5.6 (a)]. Memory, intelligence, reasoning and other mental activities including response to stimuli are controlled by the cerebrum.

Tech Info

Magnetic resonance imaging (MRI) is a technique used to identify the response of different parts of the brain to external stimuli.

- **Cerebellum**: It is located below the cerebrum [Fig. 5.6 (b)]. This part of the brain controls and coordinates muscular movements of the body and also maintains the balance of the body.
- **Brain stem**: It connects the brain to the spinal cord. The brain stem helps to regulate breathing, controls heartbeat and all the involuntary movements.

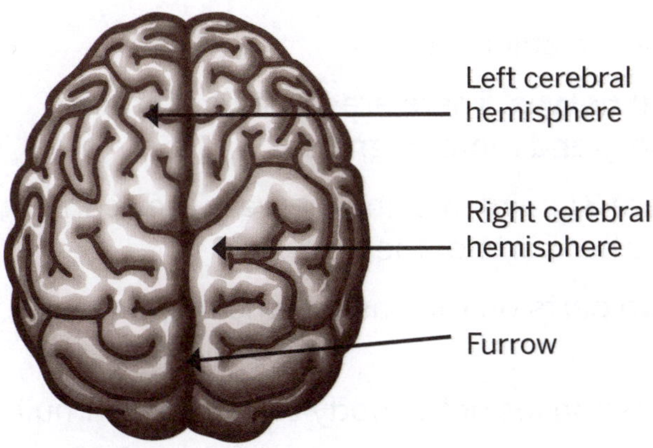

(a) Top view

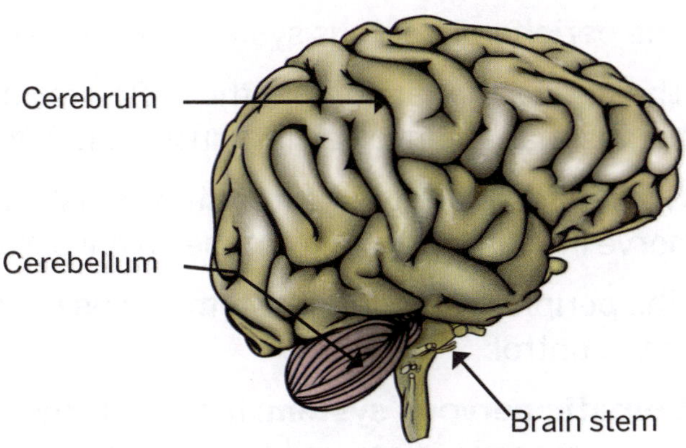

(b) Side view

▲ Fig. 5.6 Human brain

Spinal cord: Spinal cord is the continuation of the brain stem. It is found inside the vertebral column [Fig. 5.7 (a) and (b)]. The spinal cord transmits impulses from the organs of the body to the brain and from the brain to the other body parts.

A cross section of the spinal cord [Fig. 5.7 (c)] looks like a butterfly with a canal-like structure in the middle. This canal is known as the **central canal**. It contains cerebrospinal fluid. It is surrounded by an H-shaped area called **grey matter**, made up of cell bodies of the neurons. The outer area surrounding the grey matter is called **white matter**. It is made up of nerve fibres.

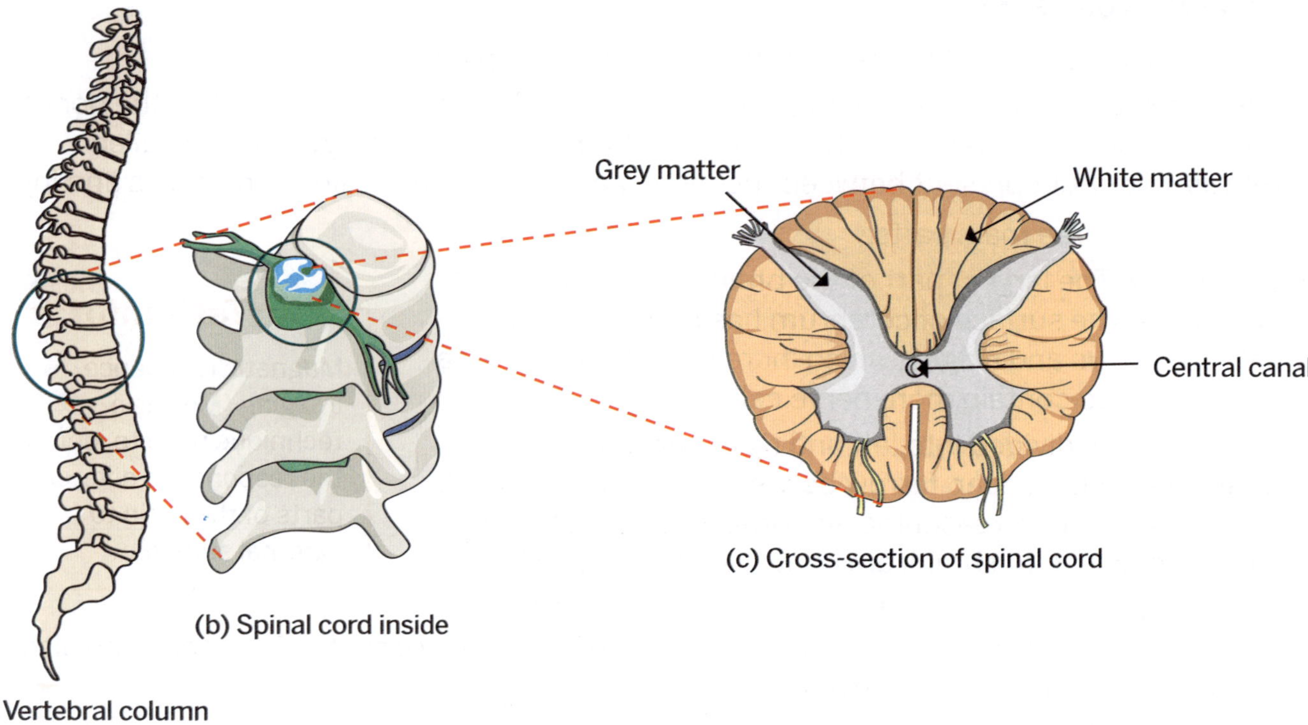

▲ Fig. 5.7 Structure of spinal cord

Peripheral Nervous System

The peripheral nervous system consists of the cranial and spinal nerves.

The nerves that arise from the brain are called **cranial nerves**. There are 12 pairs of cranial nerves that are involved in transmission of both sensory and motor signals.

Spinal nerves originate from the spinal cord. There are 31 pairs of spinal nerves. They carry nerve impulses to and from the spinal cord to all the other parts of the body.

The peripheral nervous system can be divided into two parts on the basis of the responses they control:

Somatic nervous system: It controls the voluntary responses of the body to external stimuli. These responses are under our conscious control.

Autonomous nervous system: It controls the involuntary functions of the internal organs of the body. This is not under our conscious control. This nervous system is further subdivided into two types:

- **Sympathetic nervous system**: It prepares the body for intense physical activity, commonly referred to as **fight or flight response**.

- **Parasympathetic nervous system**: It relaxes the body and slows down many functions that require more energy, commonly called **rest and digest response**.

  Both these systems control the same group of body functions, but they have opposite effects on the functions they regulate. For example, the sympathetic nervous system increases heart rate, whereas parasympathetic nervous system slows it down.

Revision Zone

Write T for True and F for False.

1. Messages passed through the nervous system are called nerve impulses.
2. Brain stem controls the balance of the body.
3. The brain is the only component of the central nervous system.
4. Spinal cord is protected by the vertebral column.

Keywords

Excretion: removal of waste products produced due to life processes from the body

Dendrite: the branched structures arising from the cell body of a neuron

Myelin sheath: a layer of insulation around the axon of a neuron

Nerve impulse: the messages passed through the nervous system

Meninges: protective layers located between the brain and the skull

In a Nutshell

- In humans, waste products are released from the body through the lungs, kidney and skin.
- Urinary tract infection and kidney stones are some of the common disorders found in the excretory system.
- The nervous system and endocrine system help in the control and coordination of our body.
- Neuron is the fundamental unit of the nervous system.
- Central nervous system consists of the brain and the spinal cord.
- The brain consists of cerebrum, cerebellum and brain stem.
- Brain stem continues to form the spinal cord.
- The cross-section of the spinal cord shows an H-shaped dark area called grey matter surrounded by a lighter region called white matter.
- The peripheral nervous system consists of 12 pairs of cranial and 31 pairs of spinal nerves, which carry impulses to and from the central nervous system to various parts of the body.

Mind Map

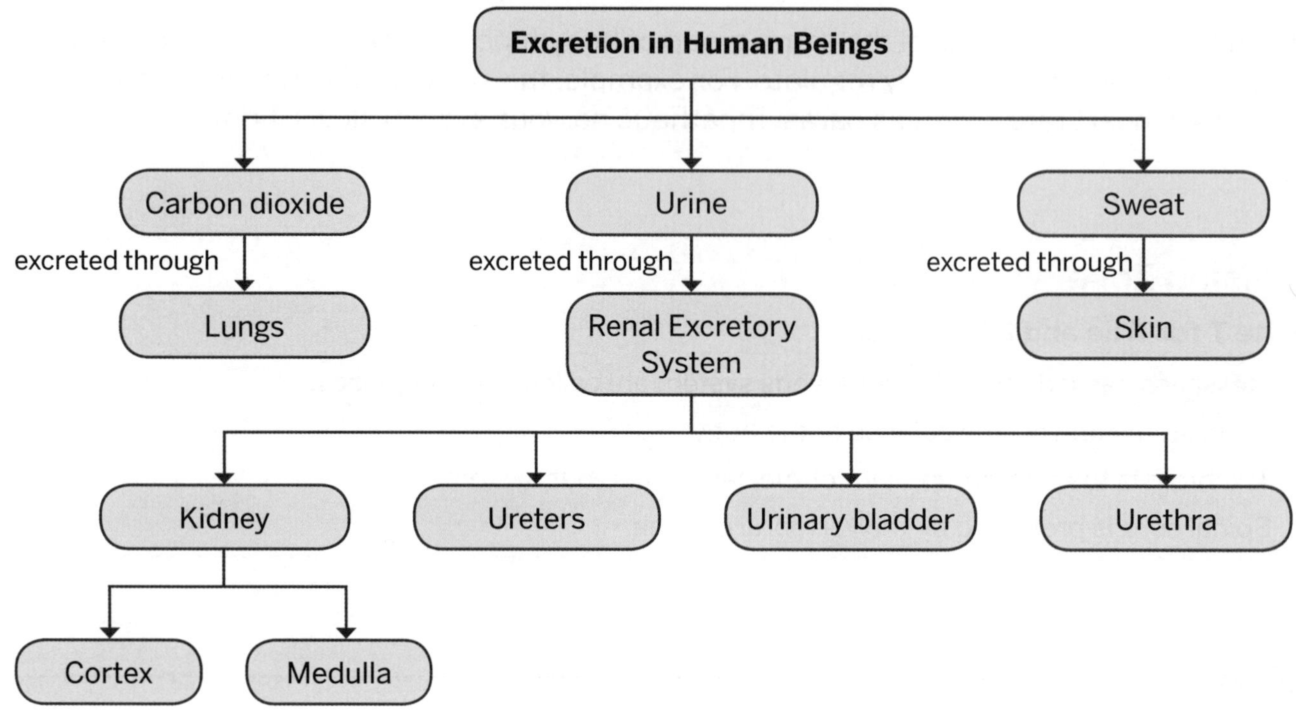

Excretion in Human Beings
Carbon dioxide
excreted through
Lungs
Urine
excreted through
Renal Excretory System
Sweat
excreted through
Skin
Kidney
Ureters
Urinary bladder
Urethra
Cortex
Medulla

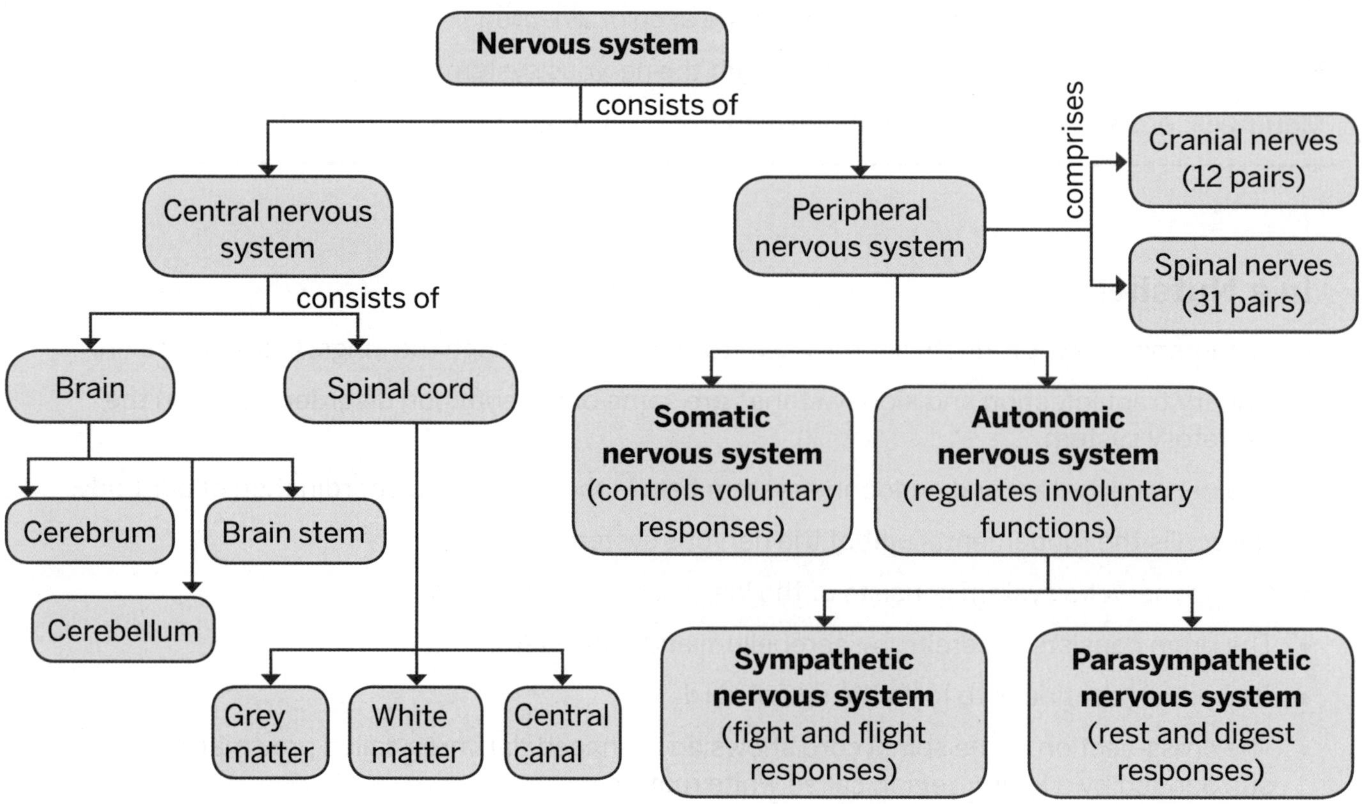

Nervous system
consists of
Central nervous system
consists of
Brain
Spinal cord
Cerebrum
Brain stem
Cerebellum
Grey matter
White matter
Central canal
Peripheral nervous system
comprises
Cranial nerves (12 pairs)
Spinal nerves (31 pairs)
Somatic nervous system (controls voluntary responses)
Autonomic nervous system (regulates involuntary functions)
Sympathetic nervous system (fight and flight responses)
Parasympathetic nervous system (rest and digest responses)

Exercise

1 Choose the correct answer for each of the following.

a. Which of the following is the passage to move urine out of the body?
   i. Ureter   ii. Urinary bladder
   iii. Urethra   iv. Anus

b. Which of the following is the structural and functional unit of a kidney?
   i. Nephron   ii. Neuron
   iii. Kidney   iv. Ureter

c. The message carried by the nervous system is called
   i. stimulus   ii. sensation
   iii. response   iv. impulse

d. The junction where one nerve cell connects to another is called
   i. axon   ii. dendron
   iii. synapse   iv. dendrite

e. The function of the myelin sheath is
   i. receiving impulse
   ii. insulating the axon
   iii. generating impulse
   iv. None of these

f. Which part of the brain maintains the balance of the body?
   i. Cerebellum   ii. Cerebrum
   iii. Brain stem   iv. None of these

g. The H-shaped structure in the spinal cord is called
   i. grey matter   ii. white matter
   iii. central canal   iv. black matter

h. There are ________ of spinal nerves.
   i. 31 pairs   ii. 13 pairs
   iii. 12 pairs   iv. 24 pairs

2 Fill in the blanks.

a. The longitudinal section of a kidney shows a dark outer region called ________ (medulla/cortex)

b. ________ (Urinating/Sweating) maintains the temperature of the body by reducing the body's temperature.

c. Waste product of respiration is ________ (CO_2/O_2)

d. Infection in the lower part of the urinary tract is also called ________ infection (bladder/kidney).

e. The ________ (sensory/motor) neuron transmits impulses from the brain and spinal cord to other parts of the body.

f. Grey matter and white matter are parts of the ________ (brain/spinal cord).

g. The ________ (somatic/autonomous) nervous system controls the voluntary responses of the body to external stimuli.

3 Write T for True and F for False.

a. Urine and sweat are the only two waste products formed in the human body.

b. From the ureter the urine moves to the urethra.

c. Axon is insulated and protected by nodes of Ranvier.

d. Afferent and efferent neurons are connected by interneurons.

e. Cerebellum is the largest part of the brain.

f. The white matter in spinal cord is made of cell bodies of neurons.

g. The nerves that arise from the brain are called cranial nerves.

h. The brain and the spinal cord form the peripheral nervous system.

4 Differentiate between the following.

a. Afferent and efferent neurons

b. Cerebrum and cerebellum

c. Central nervous system and peripheral nervous system
d. Somatic nervous system and autonomous nervous system
e. Sympathetic nervous system and parasympathetic nervous system

5 Answer the following questions in brief.

a. Define excretion. Name the excretory organs of a human body.
b. Which part of the kidney is called the structural and functional unit of the kidney?
c. What are the organs of the renal excretory system?
d. What are the three types of neurons?
e. Give the structure of a neuron with the help of a diagram.
f. Describe the structure of the spinal cord.
g. Explain the autonomic nervous system.

6 Answer the following questions in detail.

a. Describe the renal excretory system with the help of a diagram.
b. Describe the structure of a human kidney.
c. What are the common excretory disorders found in human? Explain.
d. Write a note on the human brain, its structure and functions.
e. Describe the peripheral nervous system.

7 Think and answer.

What happens when you accidentally touch a hot container?

(Hint: Reflex action)

8 Label the diagrams given below.

a.

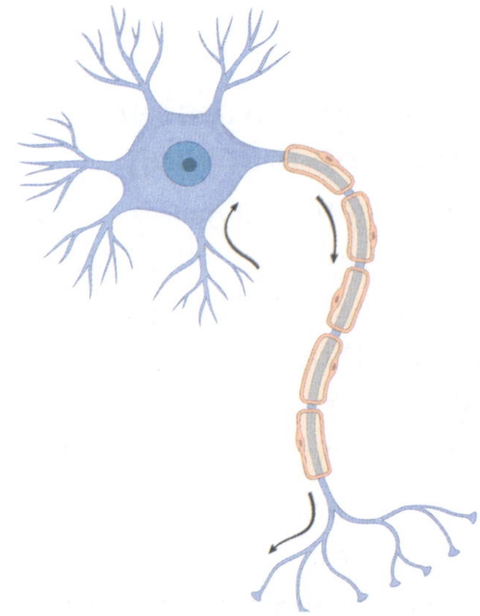

b.

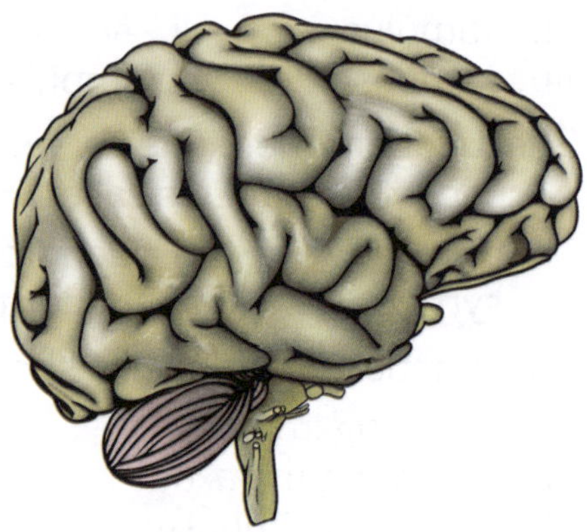

9 Project

Prepare a model of human excretory system with biodegradable materials and display it in the class.

10 In the Library

Refer your library books and make a report on diseases of the lungs like bronchitis and asthma.

Worksheet

Subject Integration

❶ **Draw a labelled diagram of the human kidney in the space given below.**

❷ **Identify the type of nerve cell (sensory neuron, motor neuron or interneuron) shown in the diagram below. Also, label its parts.**

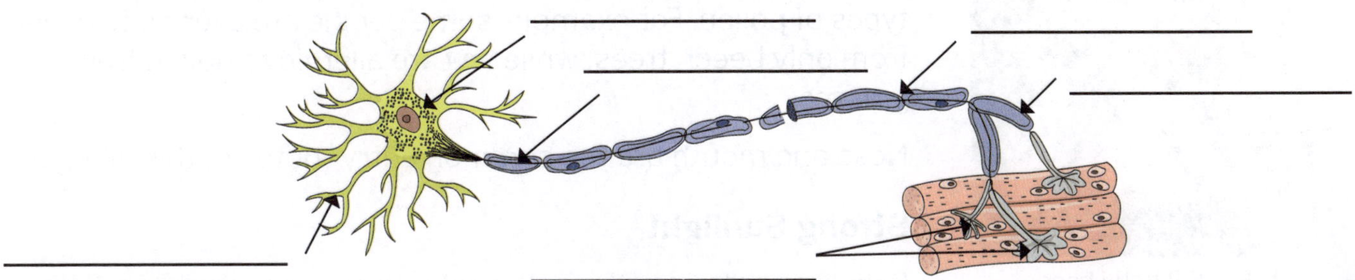

Health and Hygiene: Allergy

6

What I shall learn

- Allergy and allergens
- Symptoms produced by allergens
- Seasonal or perennial allergy
- Precautions to be taken for allergy

▲ Fig. 6.1 Pollen grains

▲ Fig. 6.2 Itchy hands

Introduction

Hypersensitive immune response to substances that either enter or come in contact with the body is called an **allergy**. It occurs when one's immune system reacts to a substance in the environment.

The substances that cause an allergic reaction are called **allergens**. Some examples of allergens are dust mites, pets, pollen, insects, moulds, foods and some medicines.

A substance which is an allergen to one person may not be an allergen to another.

Common Allergens and Their Entry Routes

Dust Mites

Dust mites are the most common cause of allergy from dust. They live and multiply in warm and humid places. Dust mites are a common cause of asthma in children. They float into the air when someone vacuums, walks on a carpet or disturbs bedding, and they settle once the disturbance is over.

Nose and mouth are the common entry routes of dust mites.

Pollen Grains

Pollens are fine coarse powdery substance consisting of pollen grains, which are the male gametes produced by trees, grasses, flowers and weeds. People can be allergic to different types of pollen. For example, some people are allergic to pollen from only beech trees; while few are allergic to pollen from grasses.

Nose and mouth are the common entry routes of this allergen.

Strong Sunlight

Itchy red rashes occur on the skin when exposed to sunlight; this condition is often known as **sun allergy**. Polymorphic light eruption (PLE) is the most common form of sun allergy. It is also known as sun poisoning. In PLE, when light hits the skin it causes slight changes in the skin cells and the individual's body reacts against these changes to fight them off. This causes itchy spots or blisters.

Skin is the only route for the entry of this allergen.

Food Items

Some food items that account for about 90 per cent of the allergic reactions are eggs, milk, peanuts, tree nuts (almonds, cashews, walnuts, etc.), fish, shellfish, wheat, soy, sesame and mustard seeds. Symptoms may involve the skin, the gastrointestinal tract, the cardiovascular system and the respiratory tract.

A type of delayed food allergy reaction seen in infants is food protein-induced enterocolitis syndrome (FPIES). It is a severe gastrointestinal reaction that generally occurs two to six hours after consuming milk, soy and certain grains.

This allergen enters into the body through mouth.

▲ Fig. 6.3 Food allergens

Revision Zone

Match the following.

1. Peanuts	a. Male gametes from flowers
2. Polymorphic light eruption	b. Delayed food allergy in infants
3. Dust mites	c. Food allergen
4. Food protein-induced enterocolitis syndrome	d. Asthma in children
5. Pollens	e. Sun allergy

Symptoms of an Allergic Reaction

When an allergic person comes in contact with an allergen, an allergic reaction occurs. When the allergens enter the body, it triggers a response by releasing certain chemical substances called histamine. This results in swelling and inflammation, which is extremely irritating and uncomfortable.

Some symptoms commonly shown by different categories of allergens are given below:

- Allergens that enter from nose and/or eyes trigger symptoms such as conjunctivitis (inflammation of the eyes that cause them to become red and watery) and allergic rhinitis (inflammation of the mucous membrane that lines the nose).
- Allergens that enter through skin trigger symptoms such as eczema and hives, and that enter into the lungs cause asthma.
- Food allergens trigger symptoms like vomiting and/or stomach cramps, shortness of breath, wheezing, repetitive cough, hoarse throat, swelling of the tongue and lips, pale or blue colouring of skin, dizziness or feeling faint and anaphylaxis.

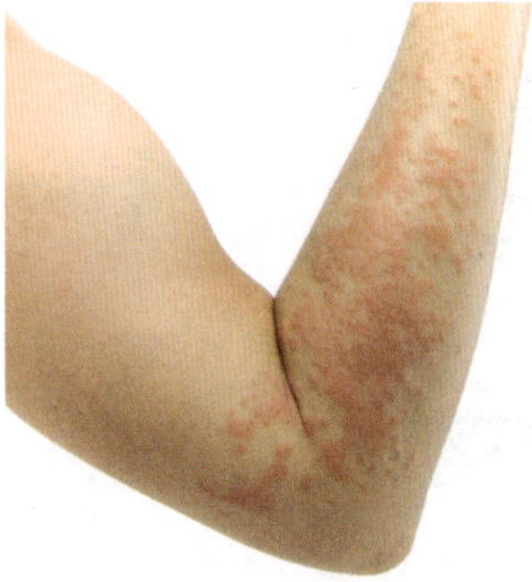

▲ Fig. 6.4 Hives

▲ Fig. 6.5 Conjunctivitis

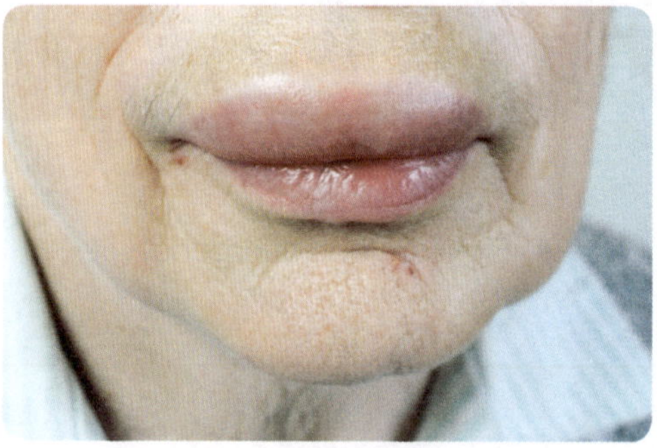

▲ Fig. 6.6 Swollen lips

Anaphylaxis: Anaphylaxis is a severe allergic reaction that can come on within minutes of exposure to an allergen to which a person might have been exposed once before. This is a condition where the breathing/heart rate of an individual is impaired by a sudden drop in the blood pressure. It can be fatal if not treated at the earliest.

Do You Know?

Not everyone who experiences symptoms after eating certain food items has food allergy. For example, some people experience an itchy mouth and throat after eating a raw or uncooked fruit or vegetable. This may indicate oral allergy syndrome – a reaction to pollen, not to the food.

Types of Allergy

Allergies can be categorized into the following types:

- **Non-seasonal** or **perennial allergy** can occur any time of the year. Dust, dust mites, dander (small particles or scales of hair or feathers, dandruff, etc.), saliva from dogs and cats and moulds are some common perennial allergens.
- **Seasonal allergy** occurs at a particular time every year. This type of allergy usually occurs during the season when the pollen from plants is dispersed. Trees (especially in the spring), grasses, plants like hay, wheat and corn (mostly present in the summer) and herbaceous plants during the end of summer and in fall (ragweed) are some of the common seasonal allergens. Seasonal allergy due to pollens is also called **hay fever**. Symptoms of hay fever include sneezing, runny nose and watery eyes due to inflammation of the mucous membranes of the eyes and nose.

Another form of seasonal allergy is caused during the rainy season due to the spores released by moulds.

▲ Fig. 6.7 Moulds growing on old buildings

▲ Fig. 6.8 Ragweed

Precautions and Care

Some of the precautions and care to be taken by a person prone to allergies are tabulated below.

Allergies	Precautions and Care
Dust allergy	• Get rid of carpets and dust-collecting furniture, such as stuffed chairs, periodically. • Wash sheets, pillow cases and bedspreads in hot water. • Wash floors regularly. • Keep the ambient humidity level low. • Install a high-efficiency air filter. • Go for allergy shots if the allergy persists for a long time.

Allergies	Precautions and Care
Pollen allergy	• Keep doors and windows closed. • Do not mow the lawn or go to places where your allergen can be found (e.g., parks and other areas with plants). • Do not dry your clothes on the clothesline. • Wear sunglasses whenever you are outside. • Control some symptoms with over-the-counter medication like decongestants and antihistamines (eye drops, nasal spray and oral medication). • Consult an allergist for prescription medications.
Skin allergy	• Always cover the body before going out in the sun. • Apply sunscreen lotions on the exposed parts of the body before going out. • Consult an allergist immediately in case of any itch or blister.
Food allergy	• Be extra careful when eating in restaurants. • Epinephrine (adrenaline) is the first-line treatment for anaphylaxis. • Consult a doctor for treatment.

Keywords

Allergy: hypersensitive response of the body to certain substances

Allergen: any substance that causes allergy

Pollen: fine coarse powdery substance consisting of pollen grains

Conjunctivitis: inflammation of the conjunctiva of the eye

Allergic rhinitis: inflammation in the nose in response to an allergen

Anaphylaxis: an acute allergic hypersensitive reaction to an allergen

Perennial allergy: allergy which can occur all year

Seasonal allergy: allergy which occurs at the same time every year

In a Nutshell

- Hypersensitive immune response to substances that either enter or come in contact with the body is called an allergy.
- Allergy occurs when ones immune system reacts to a substance in the environment that is harmless for most people.
- Substances that cause an allergic reaction are called as allergens.
- Some allergens are dust mites, pets, pollen, insects, moulds, foods and some medicines.
- A substance which is an allergen to one person may not be an allergen to another.
- Allergy can be prevented by avoiding the allergens through different measures.

Mind Map

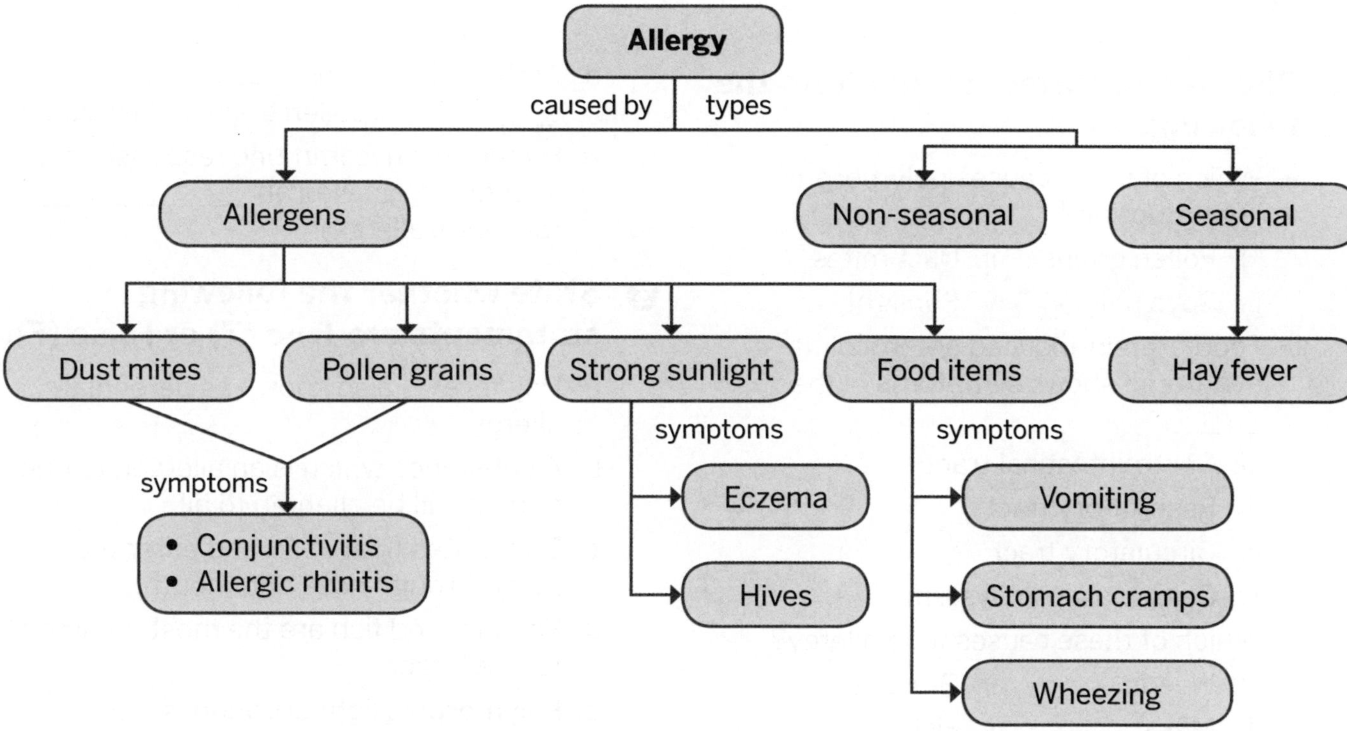
Allergy
caused by
types
Allergens
Non-seasonal
Seasonal
Dust mites
Pollen grains
Strong sunlight
Food items
Hay fever
symptoms
Conjunctivitis
Allergic rhinitis
symptoms
Eczema
Hives
symptoms
Vomiting
Stomach cramps
Wheezing

Exercise

1 Choose the correct option from the following.

a. Which of these causes polymorphic light eruption?
   i. Pollen grains   ii. Dust mites
   iii. Soya milk   iv. Sunlight

b. Food protein-induced enterocolitis syndrome shows symptoms in the ______.
   i. Gastrointestinal tract
   ii. Respiratory tract
   iii. Circulatory tract
   iv. Cardiovascular system

c. Which of these causes food allergy?
   i. Weeds   ii. Grasses
   iii. Mites   iv. Fish

d. Eczema and hives are the symptoms seen in which of these organs?
   i. Skin   ii. Eyes
   iii. Stomach   iv. Lungs

e. Which of these is NOT a symptom of food allergy?
   i. Vomiting
   ii. Pale colouring of skin
   iii. Anaphylaxis
   iv. Asthma

2 Fill in the blanks using the correct words.

a. Ragweed causes ______________ allergy. (seasonal/ perennial)

b. Epinephrine is the first line of treatment for ______________. (asthma/ anaphylaxis)

c. Pollen allergy can be controlled by ______________an over the counter medicine. (antihistamine/adrenaline)

d. Asthma in children is caused by ___________. (pollen grains/ dust mites)

e. Hypersensitive immune response to a substance is called an ______________. (allergen/allergy)

3 State whether the following statements are True (T) or False (F).

a. Hay fever is also known as perennial allergy.

b. A substance which is an allergen to one person will be allergen to all.

c. Dust mites float in air and enter the body through nose and mouth.

d. Peanuts and fish are the most common food allergens.

e. Polymorphic light eruption is also known as sun poisoning.

4 Define the following terms.

a. Allergy

b. Allergens

c. Polymorphic light eruption

d. Anaphylaxis

e. Pollen grains

5 Answer the following questions briefly.

a. Write a note on food allergens.

b. How does strong sunlight act as an allergen?

c. Write the difference between allergy and allergen.

d. Write a note on different types of allergy.

e. List the precautionary measures to be taken against a pollen allergy.

6 Answer the following questions.

a. Write a note on allergic reactions and its symptoms.

b. List different types of allergens and explain any two.

c. What are the precautionary measures to be taken against dust and food allergy?

7 HOTS (Higher Order Thinking Skills)

Our immune system may be referred to small bands of Japanese "holdout" soldiers after World War II. Find out why? (Hint: Mistakenly fighting against innocent)

8 In the laboratory

Observe a permanent slide of pollen grains and dust mites that causes allergy.

9 Identify the symptoms of allery shown in the pictures given below.

a.

b.

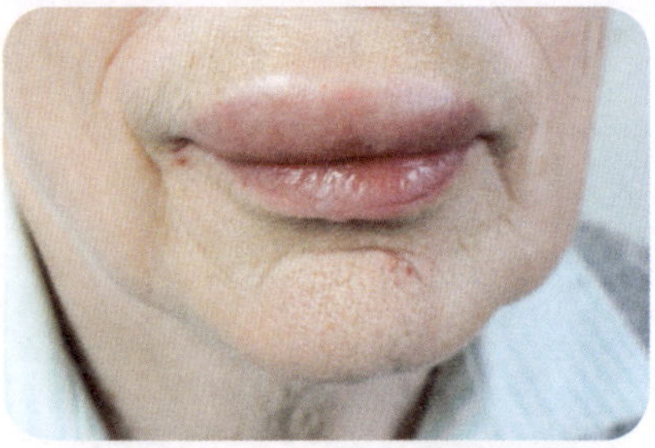

c.

Worksheet

1 Subject Integration

Your school is celebrating an Allergy Awareness week. Design your own poster to be pasted on the school notice board in the space given below and write a catchy slogan beneath it.

____

2 Life Skills

Health awareness: Our health is affected by a variety of factors. Among these factors, our lifestyle plays a huge role in how healthy we are. From what we eat and drink, to how much we exercise, everything effects our health. But being aware of what is good for our health and what isn't helps us make the right lifestyle choices.

List five healthy lifestyle choices you will make to keep yourself fit and protect yourself from diseases.

a. ______________________________

b. ______________________________

c. ______________________________

d. ______________________________

e. ______________________________

Assessments

Assessment 1 (Chapters 1-3)

Maximum Marks: 40

1 Choose the correct answer for each of the following. (5 × 1 = 5)

a. Kingdom, Phylum and Family are
   i. characteristics of an organism
   ii. names of species
   iii. taxonomical ranks
   iv. different genera

b. Which of the following is a human parasite?
   i. Lobster
   ii. Wasp
   iii. Tapeworm
   iv. Spider

c. Which of the following plant tissues conducts minerals and water?
   i. Parenchyma
   ii. Phloem
   iii. Collenchyma
   iv. Xylem

d. Cells of which of the following tissues have a basement membrane?
   i. Nervous tissue
   ii. Epithelial tissue
   iii. Muscular tissue
   iv. None of these

e. Which of these have organs called suckers?
   i. Oyster
   ii. Slug
   iii. Starfish
   iv. Centipede

2 Fill in the blanks. (5 × 1 = 5)

a. Dendrons branch out to form __________ (dendrites/axon).

b. False feet in Amoeba are also known as _________ (pseudopodia/flagella).

c. Parrots have hollow bones, wings and __________ (streamlined body/webbed feet) that help them to fly.

d. Blood is a __________ (fluid/fibrous) connective tissue.

e. ________ (Kingdom/ Species) is the highest rank in taxonomy.

3 Write T for True and F for False. (5 × 1 = 5)

a. Smooth muscles are found in the internal organs of the body.

b. Aristotle gave the five kingdom classification.

c. Newts belong to the class Reptilia.

d. Cells in the apical meristem divide actively.

e. Lateral meristem causes growth in length.

4 Give reasons for the following. (5 × 2 = 10)

a. Voluntary skeletal muscles work in pairs to bring about movement.

b. Plants stop growing when the apical meristem is removed.

c. Cardiac muscles do not get fatigued in the lifetime of an organism.

d. Sclerenchyma cells do not grow.

e. Adipose tissues insulate the body.

5 Answer the following questions in brief. (5 × 3 = 15)

a. Write a note on supporting tissues in plants.

b. What are the common characteristics of Platyhelminthes?

c. Monkeys belong to which class of vertebrates? Give the characteristic features of the class.

d. Explain with an experiment the structure of stomata.

e. Write a note on skeletal tissues.

Assessment 2 (Chapters 4-6)

Maximum Marks: 40

1 Choose the correct answer for each of the following. (5 × 1 = 5)

a. Involuntary nervous system is also known as
   i. autonomous nervous system
   ii. somatic nervous system
   iii. cranial nervous system
   iv. spinal nervous system

b. Which of these is not a characteristic allergic reaction of hay fever?
   i. Red watery eyes
   ii. Itchy and runny nose
   iii. Scaly rashes on skin
   iv. Continuous sneezing

c. Which of these is NOT a product of photosynthesis?
   i. Carbon dioxide
   ii. Oxygen
   iii. Water
   iv. Glucose

d. How many molecules of carbon dioxide are formed at the end of anaerobic respiration?
   i. 2 molecules
   ii. 4 molecules
   iii. 6 molecules
   iv. 8 molecules

e. One of these factors does not affect the rate of photosynthesis.
   i. Light
   ii. Water
   iii. Oxygen
   iv. Temperature

2 Fill in the blanks. (5 × 1 = 5)

a. The pores present in the leaves of plants are called (guard cells/stomata).

b. In aerobic respiration, oxidation of glucose releases ________ (38 ATP/2 ATP) molecules.

c. The nervous system and ________ (excretory/endocrine) system helps in control and coordination of the body.

d. Pollens are the ________ (female/male) gametes produced from the flowers.

e. ____________ (Stomata/Chlorophyll) absorbs sunlight and converts it into chemical energy.

3 Write T for True and F for False. (5 × 1 = 5)

a. A nerve cell is also called a nephron.

b. Asthma is characterized by difficulty in breathing.

c. Plants perform only photosynthesis during the daytime.

d. More energy is released during anaerobic respiration than during aerobic respiration.

e. Availability of water increases the rate of photosynthesis.

4 Give reasons for the following. (5 × 2 = 10)

a. The surface of cerebrum has many folding called furrows and ridges.

b. Temperature above 30°C stops the process of photosynthesis.

c. Exposure of skin to strong sunlight may cause sun poisoning.

d. Muscle cells switch between aerobic and anaerobic respiration.

e. Plants need sunlight to prepare food.

5 Answer the following questions in brief. (5 × 3 = 15)

a. Write a short note on anaphylaxis.

b. Write a short note on urinary tract infection.

c. What is respiration? How do plants respire?

d. Explain the role of CO_2 as a factor affecting the process of photosynthesis.

e. Explain the structure of the human brain.